CHAPTER & *verse*

AN INTERACTIVE APPROACH TO LITERATURE

EDUCATION
WEAVER

JOHN McRAE & LUISA PANTALEONI

OXFORD UNIVERSITY PRESS

Oxford University Press, Walton Street, Oxford OX2 6DP

Oxford
New York Toronto Melbourne Auckland
Petaling Jaya Singapore Hong Kong Tokyo
Delhi Bombay Madras Calcutta Karachi
Nairobi Dar es Salaam Cape Town

and associated companies in
Berlin Ibadan

Oxford and Oxford English are trade marks
of Oxford University Press

ISBN 0 19 421713 2
© Oxford University Press 1990

First impression 1990
Second impression 1991

Printed in Hong Kong

ACKNOWLEDGEMENTS

The authors and publishers are grateful for permission to use the following copyright material:

Isaac Asimov: 'True Love' Copyright © 1977 by The American Way from *The Complete Robot*. Reprinted by permission of Doubleday, a division of Bantam, Doubleday, Dell Publishing Group, Inc.
W. H. Davies: 'Leisure' from *The Complete Poems of W.H. Davies*. Reprinted by permission of Jonathan Cape Ltd. on behalf of the Executors of the W.H. Davies Estate.
Graham Greene: from *A Burnt - Out Case* (William Heinemann Ltd. & The Bodley Head Ltd.) Reprinted by permission of Laurence Pollinger Ltd.
Langston Hughes: 'I, Too' from *Selected Poems of Langston Hughes*. Reprinted by permission of Random House Inc.
Shirley Jackson: *Charles* reprinted by permission of A.M. Heath & Co. Ltd. on behalf of the estate of Shirley Jackson.
George MacBeth: 'Pavan for an Unborn Infanta' from *Collected Poems* (Macmillan, 1971). Reprinted by permission of Anthony Sheil Associates for the author.
Roger McGough: '40 – Love' from *Modern Poets 10* (Penguin Books Ltd.). Reprinted by permission of A.D. Peters & Co. Ltd.
Louis MacNeice: 'Prayer Before Birth' from *Collected Poems* (Faber). Reprinted by permission of David Higham Associates Ltd.
Edwin Morgan: 'Space Poem: Off Course', 'Chinese Cat', 'The Loch Ness Monster's Song', 'Siesta of a Hungarian Snake' and 'When You Go' from *Poems of Thirty Years* (1982). Reprinted by permission of Carcanet Press Ltd.
George Orwell: from *Keep the Aspidistra Flying* and *1984*. Reprinted by permission of A.M. Heath Ltd. on behalf of the estate of the late Sonia Brownwell Orwell and Martin Secker & Warburg.
Ezra Pound: 'Erat Hora' and 'Ite' from *Collected Shorter Poems*. Reprinted by permission of Faber & Faber Ltd.
Craig Raine: 'A Martian Sends a Postcard Home' © Craig Raine 1979. Reprinted by permission of Oxford University Press.
Alastair Reid: 'To a Child at the Piano' from *Weathering: Poems and Translations*, copyright Alastair Reid (Canongate 1979). Reprinted by permission of the author.
Siegfried Sassoon: 'Everyone Sang' from *Collected Poems*. Reprinted by permission of G.T. Sassoon.
Stevie Smith: 'Not Waving but Drowning' from *The Collected Poems of Stevie Smith* (Penguin Modern Classics). Reprinted by permission of James MacGibbon, Literary Executor.
Muriel Spark: from *The Prime of Miss Jean Brodie* (Macmillan, 1961). Reprinted by permission of David Higham Associates Ltd.
John Steinbeck: from *Of Mice and Men*. Reprinted by permission of William Heinemann Ltd.
Evelyn Waugh: from *Decline and Fall* (Chapman & Hall Ltd.) Reprinted by permission of A. D. Peters & Co. Ltd.

William Carlos Williams: 'This is Just to Say' from *The Collected Poems 1909 –1939*, edited by E. Walton Litz and Christopher MacGowan (1987). Reprinted by permission of Carcanet Press Ltd.
Virginia Woolf: from *Orlando*. Reprinted by permission of The Hogarth Press on behalf of the estate of the author.

The publishers have been unable to trace and would be pleased to hear from the copyright holders of 'The Well-Wrought Urn' by Irving Layton.

The publishers would also like to thank the following for their permission to reproduce photographs:

Ardea; The Bodleian Library M. Adds. 1068 d6., 280 c 253. plate 3; Bridgeman Art Library for 'Persistence of Memory', 1931 by Salvador Dali, Demart Pro Arte BV/ Dacs 1989 and 'The Scream', 1893 by Edvard Munch, Nasjonalgalleriet, Oslo; Dickens House; Catherine Ashmore Dominic Photography; M. C. Escher Heirs/Cordon Art - Baarn - Holland; Mary Evans Picture Library; The Kobal Collection; The Mansell Collection; 'Welcome Back' 1958 by Ronald Searle from *The Complete Molesworth* by Geoffrey Willans and Ronald Searle (published by Pavilion Books) reprinted by permission of Tessa Sayle Agency.

and the following, whose voices are heard on the cassette:

Ian Bamforth; Judy Bennett; Timothy Bentinck; Roger Blake; Garrick Hagon; Frances Jeater; Deborah Makepeace; Richard Mitchley; Kenneth Shanley; Susan Sheridan; Jill Shilling.

This book was first published, in an expanded version, as *Words on the Page* by La Nuova Italia and Oxford University Press, Firenze and Oxford, 1985 (second edition 1986).

The authors wish to thank Simon Murison-Bowie, Jeremy Hunter, Susan Sharp, Ron Carter, and Paola Silvestrini, for help and encouragement at various stages of the project. A special word of thanks goes to Norman Whitney for suggesting the title.

CONTENTS

INTRODUCTION

Chapter and Verse brings imaginative texts within the reach of students learning English who may be at any stage from intermediate upwards. As the title suggests, the book contains a mixture of prose and poetry. The texts are usually extracts from longer pieces but there are also complete short stories, poems, scenes from plays, and a variety of short quotations. We have tried to offer a mixture of texts from different periods, in different styles, on a range of different subjects, which students are invited to read, analyse and refer to when verbalizing their responses.

Organization of the materials

Each of the ten chapters contains four to six main texts, which are linked thematically. They also include pictures, quotations, and other related material which help the reader to explore the central theme in greater detail.

In general the earlier chapters are less demanding than the later ones, and, within the individual chapters, there is an element of grading in that the final text is always likely to be the most challenging.

First steps

Chapter and Verse provides reading texts for enjoyment and language development. On reading them, students should feel free to react and interact, both with the teacher and with each other, giving opinions and responses, challenging and discussing ideas, agreeing and disagreeing. Each chapter opens with a few questions or quotations which are designed to arouse interest in the theme. Some teachers may prefer to work on the texts straight away, but it is usually advisable to take a little time to introduce the subject, especially if students are not used to studying literature in this way.

Texts, exercises, teaching

Most of the texts are recorded on the cassette (accompanied by this symbol 🔲). We strongly recommend that students, whether in class or studying alone, listen to the cassette (or to the teacher reading) while reading the text for the first time. Second and subsequent readings may be accompanied by the cassette or not. Reading and listening together add considerably to the enjoyment of the text, which we want to be one of the keynotes of the book.

It is not necessary to study all the texts in a chapter, or to work through all the chapters in the book in order. Often time constraints will mean that a whole

chapter cannot be covered in class - but students should be encouraged to read on, and perhaps to work through all or part of the exercises (using the Teacher's Notes for guidance, as necessary) in their own time. This can be both a pleasurable reading activity/language exercise, and a way of reinforcing work done in class. In preparing the materials we have found that students become enthusiastic about the process of discovering for themselves how various authors approach a range of themes, and this can encourage them to go to the full text of a work which they have read about in extract form, or to find out more about an author. In fact, a major aim of the book is to encourage students' initiative, autonomy and development by increasing their linguistic and communicative competence through classroom interaction.

Although many of the exercises are designed to help basic understanding, reading comprehension as such is *not* the main objective. *Exploitation* of what has been read, for discussion in class, for reflection or for written work is more important.

Discussion and Graffiti

These sections appear in each chapter and are deliberately presented without a heavy load of instructions: they can be used as stimuli for oral work in class or written work at home, for project work, group work, and debates. Often they are simply quotations which encapsulate aspects of the wider theme of the chapter. They can be used in any of the above ways according to individual or class needs, or they can be accepted or rejected very briefly. Some readers will be happy to regard the quotations in the Graffiti sections as more or less fitting conclusions to the subject they have been reading about, discussing and evaluating.

Tasks

The Tasks are intended principally to develop study skills in relation to what has been read. In particular they encourage students to reflect on themes and materials, to revise language and ideas, to identify key images or memorable sentences and to transfer them to other contexts. These are fundamental skills which the oral and written summaries constantly featuring in the questions accompanying the texts call for and promote. Summary skills, crucial to all post-reading activities, develop study and examination skills and contribute considerably to academic success.

Teachers may decide to leave out the Tasks if they feel that skills such as summarizing, researching into authors, etc. are not part of their objectives. However teachers who want to bring their students closer to the study of literature as a subject will probably make more use of them. Flexibility is important and tasks can be approached orally or as written work, in class or as homework, in groups or individually.

Vocabulary

When the object of the exercise is enjoyment of the imaginative use of language it may be inadvisable to aim for strict analytical rigour where vocabulary is concerned. Bearing this in mind, some texts are followed by exercises which include vocabulary work while others are not, and the reader's overall response to a text is more important than understanding every single word or even answering every single question. (We would want to avoid students reading each line struggling to look up every word.)

Suggestions for dealing with unknown words could include: listening and reading for gist in order to extract only the essential aspects of the message, or, encouraging the use of guesswork, with the recourse to a monolingual dictionary for confirmation after an initial reading.

Reaction and Creativity

Naturally, with an approach designed to involve the reader as much as possible with what is read, subjective reactions and discussion are encouraged. Very often we have left 'Open response' as the answer in the Teacher's Notes, as often there is no *correct* answer as such, and each reader's response can be equally valid. Both teachers and students should feel free to *dislike* a text, and they should also feel free to integrate their own materials with those in the book: pop songs, newspaper articles, film and video clips, texts in the students' own language, and indeed students' own creative writing can all expand the range. As soon as a student expresses a preference for one text over another, or suggests a different text to illuminate the theme, a process of critical evaluation and response is taking place - and while we are not trying to turn our students into critics, we hope that we are helping them, to be aware readers of the world around them, and creative participants in it.

Sssnnnwhufffll?

1

Here is a message – read it and try to decide where it could be left.

> This is just to say I have eaten the plums that were in the icebox and which you were probably saving for breakfast. Forgive me, they were delicious, so sweet and so cold.

1.1

Who do you think wrote the message? Why?

1.2

Can you make the message shorter? Discuss with a partner, or others in the class, what you can cut out and what you want to keep.

1.3

Do you think this message could be a poem? Discuss why or why not. Now see if you can write it to look like a poem.

1.4

Compare the poem versions around the class. Does the 'message' change from version to version, or is it always the same? What title can you give your poem?

1.5

Look closely at the last five words. What do they add to the basic message, in your opinion?

1.6

Here is a version of the message written as a poem. As you read it, compare it with your own version.

> This Is Just to Say
>
> I have eaten
> the plums
> that were in
> the icebox
> and which
> you were probably
> saving
> for breakfast
> Forgive me
> they were delicious
> so sweet
> and so cold
>
> *William Carlos Williams*

1.7

What do you think the title of this version is?

1.8

Look at the punctuation of your version: commas, full stops, capital letters. How is it different from this version, or from what you normally expect?

1.9

Is it a poem, in your opinion? Discuss why or why not.

2

THE LOCH NESS MONSTER'S SONG

Edwin Morgan plays with words and calls the result poems. Do you agree that these are poems?

> Sssnnnwhuffffll?
> Hnwhuffl hhnnwfl hnfl hfl?
> Gdroblboblhobngbl gbl gl g g g g glbgl.
> Drublhaflablhaflubhafgabhaflhafl fl fl –
> gm grawwwww grf grawf awfgm graw gm.
> Hovoplodok-doplodovok-plovodokot-doplodokosh?
> Splgraw fok fok splgrafhatchgabrlgabrl fok splfok!
> Zgra kra gka fok!
> Grof grawff gahf?
> Gombl mbl bl –
> blm plm,
> blm plm,
> blm plm,
> blp.

SPACEPOEM 3: OFF COURSE

   the golden flood   the weightless seat
   the cabin song   the pitch black
   the growing beard   the floating crumb
   the shining rendezvous   the orbit wisecrack
5 the hot spacesuit   the smuggled mouth-organ
   the imaginary somersault   the visionary sunrise
   the turning continents   the space debris
   the golden lifeline   the space walk
   the crawling deltas   the camera moon
10 the pitch velvet   the rough sleep
   the crackling headphone   the space silence
   the turning earth   the lifeline continents
   the cabin sunrise   the hot flood
   the shining spacesuit   the growing moon
15 the crackling somersault   the smuggled orbit
   the rough moon   the visionary rendezvous
   the weightless headphone   the cabin debris
   the floating lifeline   the pitch sleep
   the crawling camera   the turning silence
20 the space crumb   the crackling beard
   the orbit mouth-organ   the floating song

CHINESE CAT

p m r k g n i a o u
p m r k g n i a o
p m r k n i a o
p m r n i a o
p m r i a o
p m i a o
m i a o
m a o

SIESTA OF A HUNGARIAN SNAKE

s sz sz SZ sz SZ sz ZS zs ZS zs zs z

Edwin Morgan

2.1

What sounds are important in these texts, in your opinion? Why?

2.2

Which is the most 'serious' of these texts? Why?

2.3

Can you make a story of what has happened in *Spacepoem 3: Off Course*? What do the repeated words and noun phrases in this poem tell you?

2.4

If these poems did not each have a title, would they be just as easy to understand, or more difficult? Why?

2.5

If you like, you can now try writing texts of your own like these. See what titles the rest of the group gives them before revealing your own!

3 📟

As you read and listen to the next text, try to decide what the sounds make you think of.

AN-AN CHI-CHI
AN-AN CHI-CHI

CHI-CHI AN-AN
CHI-CHI AN-AN

CHI-AN

CHI-AN CHI-AN CHI-AN CHI-AN CHI
AN-CHI AN-CHI AN-CHI AN

CHI-AN CHI-AN CHI-AN CHI-AN CHI
AN-CHI AN-CHI AN-CHI AN

CHI-AN

AN-CHI AN-CHI AN-CHI AN
AN-CHI AN-CHI AN-CHI AN

CHI-CHI

AN-AN CHI-CHI
AN-AN CHI-CHI

CHI-CHI AN-AN
CHI-CHI AN-AN

AN-AN

AN-AN AN-AN AN-AN AN-AN

CHI-CHI CHI-CHI CHI-CHI
CHI-CHI CHI-CHI CHI-CHI

CHI-CHI

AN-AN AN-AN
AN-AN AN-AN

AN-AN AN-AN
AN-AN AN-AN

AN-AN

CHI-CHI CHI-CHI
CHI-CHI CHI-CHI

CHI-CHI CHI-CHI
CHI-CHI CHI-CHI

CHI-CHI

George MacBeth

3.1 ⎯⎯⎯⎯⎯⎯⎯⎯⎯⎯⎯⎯⎯⎯⎯⎯⎯⎯⎯⎯⎯⎯⎯⎯⎯⎯⎯⎯⎯⎯⎯

Is this nonsense – or is it about something? Compare your impressions with others in the class.

3.2 ⎯⎯⎯⎯⎯⎯⎯⎯⎯⎯⎯⎯⎯⎯⎯⎯⎯⎯⎯⎯⎯⎯⎯⎯⎯⎯⎯⎯⎯⎯⎯

Make a note of these first impressions. Are they similar to what you felt about *The Loch Ness Monster's Song* and the other Edwin Morgan texts?

3.3 ⎯⎯⎯⎯⎯⎯⎯⎯⎯⎯⎯⎯⎯⎯⎯⎯⎯⎯⎯⎯⎯⎯⎯⎯⎯⎯⎯⎯⎯⎯⎯

The writer gave this poem the title *Pavan for an Unborn Infanta*. Does this help you, or does it change the meaning of the text for you? Discuss in the class what difference the title makes to you, if any.

3.4 ⎯⎯⎯⎯⎯⎯⎯⎯⎯⎯⎯⎯⎯⎯⎯⎯⎯⎯⎯⎯⎯⎯⎯⎯⎯⎯⎯⎯⎯⎯⎯

Now the secret can be revealed – the teacher will tell you about the two characters, and their story. Does the meaning change with this new information?

3.5 ⎯⎯⎯⎯⎯⎯⎯⎯⎯⎯⎯⎯⎯⎯⎯⎯⎯⎯⎯⎯⎯⎯⎯⎯⎯⎯⎯⎯⎯⎯⎯

What sense can you now make of the words and their patterns? Does the story have a beginning/middle/end?

3.6 ⎯⎯⎯⎯⎯⎯⎯⎯⎯⎯⎯⎯⎯⎯⎯⎯⎯⎯⎯⎯⎯⎯⎯⎯⎯⎯⎯⎯⎯⎯⎯

Is the overall effect happy, sad, disappointing, or anything else?

3.7 ⎯⎯⎯⎯⎯⎯⎯⎯⎯⎯⎯⎯⎯⎯⎯⎯⎯⎯⎯⎯⎯⎯⎯⎯⎯⎯⎯⎯⎯⎯⎯

Compare the impressions you had earlier (3.2) with the new impressions and ideas you now have of the poem.

Now it's time for a real story! But this story too has a 'figured' poem in it. As you read and listen, decide what the picture poem represents.

from ALICE'S ADVENTURES IN WONDERLAND

"Mine is a long and a sad tale!" said the Mouse, turning to Alice, and sighing. "It is a long tail, certainly," said Alice, looking down with wonder at the Mouse's tail; "but why do you call it sad?" And she kept on puzzling about it while the Mouse was speaking, so that her idea of the tale was something like this: –

Fury said to
a mouse, that
he met
in the
house,
"Let us
both go
to law:
I will
prosecute
you. —
Come, I'll
take no
denial;
We must
have a
trial:
For
really
this
morning
I've
nothing
to do."
Said the
mouse to
the cur,
"Such a
trial,
dear Sir,
With no
jury or
judge,
would be
wasting
our breath."
"I'll be
judge, I'll
be jury,"
Said
cunning
old Fury:
"I'll
try the
whole
cause,
and
condemn
you
to
death."

Lewis Carroll

4.1

Write the tale in a straightforward poetic form, paying particular attention to punctuation marks. Do you agree that the story is 'sad'?

4.2

What effect does this sort of playing with words on the page have on you? For example, does it leave you indifferent, disconcerted, puzzled, irritated, amused or interested?

4.3

Here are two more examples of Carroll's concern with language. They are taken from the chapter called 'A Mad Tea-Party'. As you read and listen, decide who you sympathize with, and why.

"Why is a raven like a writing-desk?"

"Come, we shall have some fun now!" thought Alice. "I'm glad they've begun asking riddles – I believe I can guess that," she added aloud.

5 "Do you mean that you think you can find out the answer to it?" said the March Hare.

"Exactly so," said Alice.

"Then you should say what you mean," the March Hare went on.

10 "I do," Alice hastily replied; "– at least I mean what I say – that's the same thing, you know."

"Not the same thing a bit!" said the Hatter. "Why , you might just as well say that 'I see what I eat' is the same thing as 'I eat what I see'!"

15 "You might just as well say," added the March Hare, "that 'I like what I get' is the same thing as 'I get what I like'!"

"You might just as well say," added the Dormouse, which seemed to be talking in its sleep, "that 'I breathe when I sleep' is the same thing as 'I sleep when I breathe'!"

20 "It is the same thing with you," said the Hatter, and here the conversation dropped, and the party sat silent for a minute, while Alice thought over all she could remember about ravens and writing-desks, which wasn't much. [...].

"They were learning to draw," the Dormouse went on, yawning
25 and rubbing its eyes, for it was getting very sleepy; "and they
drew all manner of things – every thing that begins with an M –"
"Why with an M?" said Alice.
"Why not?" said the March Hare.
Alice was silent.
30 The Dormouse had closed its eyes by this time, and was going
off into a doze; but, on being pinched by the Hatter, it woke up
again with a little shriek, and went on: "– that begins with an M,
such as mouse-traps, and the moon, and memory, and
muchness – you know you say things are 'much of a muchness'
35 – did you ever see such a thing as a drawing of a muchness!"
"Really, now you ask me," said Alice, very much confused, "I
don't think –"
"Then you shouldn't talk," said the Hatter.

Lewis Carroll

4.4

'You should say what you mean' and 'I mean what I say' (lines 8 – 10).
Are these two phrases the same thing?

4.5

Is there an answer to the riddle in the first line? What effect does the
riddle have: **a** on Alice; **b** on you?

4.6

What do you think Alice is going to say when she says 'I don't think . . .'
(lines 36 – 37)?

4.7

"Everything that begins with an M–"
"Why with an M?" said Alice.
"Why not?" said the March Hare.

How do you feel about this exchange (lines 26 – 28)? 'Why not?' is one
of the main ideas on which the whole concept of nonsense is based. Do
you agree? Why do you think Alice was silent (line 29)?

Discussion

Do you like questions which require definitive answers or do you prefer open questions? Discuss your reactions to the texts you have read so far. Consider their special effects and meaning then discuss the points in their favour and against as listed below, ticking the ones you agree with and adding any others you can think of.

Points in favour	Points against
a thought-provoking, brain-teasing	*a* not 'real' poetry
b entertaining, amusing, light-hearted, fun	*b* puzzling, confusing, irritating
c explore language potential, the richness and depth of words, how meaning is achieved	*c* meaningless, silly
d create unexpected effects, challenges the 'ordinariness' of language communication	*d* words mean what they say: no fooling around with them!
e language conventions are being made fun of	*e* the reader is being made fun of

5 📼

Look and listen to these four texts. Then decide which, if any, of them are serious!

LIMERICKS

    a There was a young person whose history,
       Was always considered a mystery;
       She sat in a ditch, although no one knew which,
       And composed a small treatise on history.

b There was an old Person of Burton,
Whose answers were rather uncertain;
When they said, "How d'ye do?" he replied, "Who are you?"
That distressing old person of Burton.

c There was an Old Man of Cape Horn,
Who wished he had never been born;
So he sat on a chair, till he died of despair.
That dolorous Man of Cape Horn.

d There was an Old Lady of Prague,
Whose language was horribly vague.
When they said, "Are these caps?" she answered, "Perhaps!"
That oracular Lady of Prague.

Edward Lear

5.1

Write out the following limericks, providing the punctuation as well.

a There was a young lady whose chin resembled the point of a pin so she had it made sharp and purchased a harp and played several tunes with her chin.

b There was an old man in a boat who said I'm afloat I'm afloat when they said no you ain't he was ready to faint that unhappy old man in a boat.

What illustrations might accompany these two limericks?

5.2

Try to imitate the form of these limericks by writing your own. First make a list of the common features of all limericks.

First words
Number of lines
Rhythm
Rhyme

5.3

Read any of the limericks aloud, stressing the rhythm and the rhyme. Notice the tone, established by the invariable narrative signal 'There was . . .'. What sort of expectations does a beginning like this set up in the reader/listener? How do the accompanying pictures match the texts?

Graffiti

They never taste who always drink;
They always talk, who never think.

Matthew Prior

As charms are nonsense, nonsense is a charm.

Benjamin Franklin

Tasks

1 Write a verse to the tune of any popular song – alternatively, analyse the lyrics of a song you are particularly fond of and discuss whether they can be called poetry or not, and why.

2 Write a short paragraph commenting on the texts in this chapter, and reporting some points of the discussion you had in class.

*They danced by the light
of the moon*

How do you relax? Do you enjoy
doing nothing? What is the most
enjoyable thing you can imagine?
Discuss your ideas of pleasure and
enjoyment with others in the class.
Decide which is the most
appealing and which is the most
common.

1 📼

The first text is called *Leisure*.
Before you read the poem, look up
'leisure' in the dictionary. Then, as
you read, try to find the answer to
the question in the first two lines.

LEISURE

> What is this life if, full of care,
> We have no time to stand and stare.
>
> No time to stand beneath the boughs
> And stare as long as sheep or cows.
>
> 5 No time to see, when woods we pass,
> Where squirrels hide their nuts in grass.
>
> No time to see, in broad daylight,
> Streams full of stars like skies at night.
>
> No time to turn at Beauty's glance,
> 10 And watch her feet, how they can dance.
>
> No time to wait till her mouth can
> Enrich that smile her eyes began.
>
> A poor life this if, full of care,
> We have no time to stand and stare.
>
> *W. H. Davies*

1.1 _____

Have you found the poet's answer to the question? If so, do you agree
with him?

1.2 _____

What does the poet see in the streams? Are they really full of stars?

1.3

Why do you think Beauty (line 9) is spelt with a capital B? Who does 'her' refer to in line 11? Who is smiling?

1.4

What do you like to think of when you 'stand and stare'? What other words could you substitute for this expression, supposing it is not to be taken literally?

1.5

What is the poem about – in just a few words?

2 📼

THE FLY

William Blake also reflects on what makes him happy. As you read and listen, try to decide why he compares himself to a fly.

    Little Fly,
    Thy summer's play
    My thoughtless hand
    Has brush'd away.

5 Am not I
    A fly like thee?
    Or art not thou
    A man like me?

    For I dance,
10 And drink, & sing,
    Till some blind hand
    Shall brush my wing.

    If thought is life
    And strength & breath,
15 And the want
    Of thought is death;

    Then am I
    A happy fly,
    If I live
20 Or if I die.

William Blake

2.1

Blake uses some old-fashioned or archaic language, for example, 'thy' (line 2), 'thee' (line 6), 'art . . . thou' (line 7). These mean, 'your', 'you' (object), and 'are . . . you' (subject) as they would be in modern English. Substitute any other archaic words you find in the text with modern English equivalents.

2.2

Find other examples of 'poetic' language, and try to decide:

a what the word order of the first verse would be in ordinary speech

b on the meaning of 'for' (line 9) and of 'want' (line 15)

c on the meaning of 'if' (line 13) and of 'if' (lines 19 and 20)

2.3

Can you find answers to these questions?

a What happened to the fly?

b Who is 'I' in the poem?

c Did he mean to hurt the fly?

d Why are the man and the fly similar?

e What is good about life, in verse three?

f How does this view of life compare with that in the Davies poem?

2.4

Whose is the 'blind hand' in line 11? Is there a connection between 'thoughtless' (line 3) and 'want of thought' (lines 15 – 16)?

2.5

What is happiness, as expressed in this poem? Try to decide which of the following statements would best define it.

Happiness is dancing, drinking and singing.
Happiness is being like a fly.
Happiness is thought.
Happiness is not thinking.

Is the poet happy at the end of the poem? Is it easy to be happy? Think about what W. H. Davies and William Blake have to say in relation to this. Do you think these poems are simple? Or do you find more to think about as you read them several times?

2.6

Try rewriting the poems with shorter or longer lines. For example, The Fly might look like this:

'Little Fly, thy summer's play
My thoughtless hand has brush'd away.'

What differences do you find in the 'new' versions you have written?

Think about:
– the visual appearance of the words on the page
– the rhymes
– the sounds

3 📼

THE OWL AND THE PUSSYCAT

Edward Lear wrote a lot of what are called 'nonsense' poems. As you read and listen to *The Owl and the Pussycat*, decide if it really is nonsense – or is it a love story?

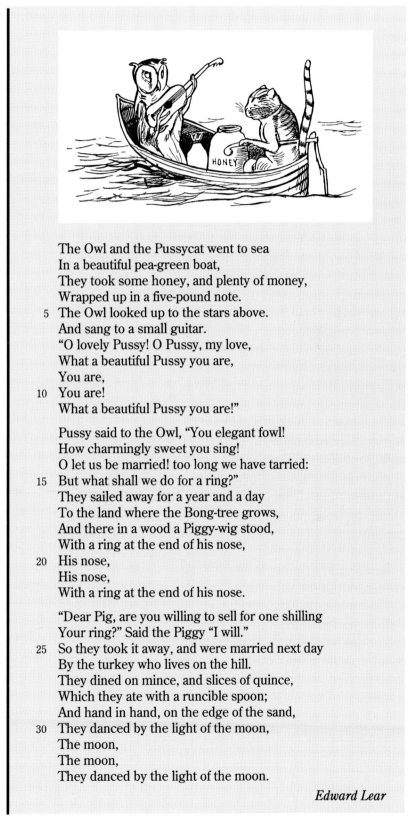

The Owl and the Pussycat went to sea
In a beautiful pea-green boat,
They took some honey, and plenty of money,
Wrapped up in a five-pound note.
5   The Owl looked up to the stars above.
And sang to a small guitar.
"O lovely Pussy! O Pussy, my love,
What a beautiful Pussy you are,
You are,
10 You are!
What a beautiful Pussy you are!"

Pussy said to the Owl, "You elegant fowl!
How charmingly sweet you sing!
O let us be married! too long we have tarried:
15 But what shall we do for a ring?"
They sailed away for a year and a day
To the land where the Bong-tree grows,
And there in a wood a Piggy-wig stood,
With a ring at the end of his nose,
20 His nose,
His nose,
With a ring at the end of his nose.

"Dear Pig, are you willing to sell for one shilling
Your ring?" Said the Piggy "I will."
25 So they took it away, and were married next day
By the turkey who lives on the hill.
They dined on mince, and slices of quince,
Which they ate with a runcible spoon;
And hand in hand, on the edge of the sand,
30 They danced by the light of the moon,
The moon,
The moon,
They danced by the light of the moon.

Edward Lear

3.1 _____

Make a list of the places the owl and the pussycat visit, and what they do in each place.

3.2 _____

How many characters are there? What does the pig do? What does the turkey do?

3.3 _____

What are the nonsensical elements of the story?

3.4 _____

See if you can find synonyms or explanations for 'fowl' (line 12), 'tarried' (line 14), 'mince' and 'quince' (line 27), 'runcible' (line 28). What do these unusual words contribute to the text?

3.5 _____

What musical effects do you find in the poem?

3.6 _____

Write the story in your own words, following the line of its development closely. Does your text look or sound like the poem?

4 _____

from THE PICTURE OF DORIAN GRAY

In Oscar Wilde's *The Picture of Dorian Gray* we find another consideration of 'happiness'. As you read Lord Henry's advice to the young Dorian Gray, pick out the things Dorian should do and should not do, to maintain his happiness.

"You really must not allow yourself to become sunburnt. It would be unbecoming."

"What can it matter?" cried Dorian Gray, laughing, as he sat down on the seat at the end of the garden.

5 "It should matter everything to you, Mr. Gray."

"Why?"

"Because you have the most marvellous youth, and youth is the one thing worth having."

"I don't feel that, Lord Henry."

10 "No, you don't feel it now. Some day, when you are old and wrinkled and ugly, when thought has seared your forehead with its lines, and passion branded your lips with its hideous fires, you will feel it, you will feel it terribly. Now, wherever you go, you charm the world. Will it always be so? . . . You have a wonderfully

15 beautiful face, Mr Gray. Don't frown. You have. And Beauty is a form of Genius – is higher, indeed, than Genius, as it needs no explanation. It is one of the great facts of the world, like sunlight, or spring-time, or the reflection in dark waters of that silver shell we call the moon. It cannot be questioned. It has its divine right

20 of sovereignty. It makes princes of those who have it. You smile? Ah! when you have lost it you won't smile . . . People say sometimes that Beauty is only superficial. That may be so. But at least it is not so superficial as Thought is. To me, Beauty is the wonder of wonders. It is only shallow people who do not judge by

25 appearances. The true mystery of the world is the visible, not the invisible . . . Yes, Mr. Gray, the gods have been good to you. But what the gods give they quickly take away. You have only a few years in which to live really, perfectly, and fully. When your youth goes, your beauty will go with it, and then you will

30 suddenly discover that there are no triumphs left for you, or have to content yourself with those mean triumphs that the memory of your past will make more bitter than defeats. Every month as it wanes brings you nearer to something dreadful. Time is jealous of you, and wars against your lilies and your roses. You will

35 become sallow, and hollow-cheeked, and dull-eyed. You will suffer horribly . . . Ah! realize your youth while you have it. Don't squander the gold of your days, listening to the tedious, trying to improve the hopeless failure, or giving away your life to the ignorant, the common, and the vulgar. These are the sickly aims,

40 the false ideals, of our age. Live! Live the wonderful life that is in you! Let nothing be lost upon you. Be always searching for new sensations. Be afraid of nothing."

Oscar Wilde

4.1

'Youth' and 'beauty' could be seen as the key words of this passage. How do they relate to Dorian's happiness?

4.2

Do you agree with the sentiments Lord Henry expresses when he says "Live! Live the wonderful life that is in you!" (lines 40 – 41)? Is such a 'philosophy of happiness' possible in our present-day world?

4.3

Pick out expressions of time in the text. Which are positive, and which negative?

4.4

Why should Dorian not get sunburnt (line 1)? Do you think a suntan is beautiful or do you prefer, like Lord Henry, a pale complexion? What makes a person good-looking, in your opinion?

4.5

Which expressions do you find the most realistic and true, and which the most exaggerated, in the passage? On the whole which aspect predominates, the realistic or the exaggerated?

4.6

Do you imagine Lord Henry is older or younger than Dorian? Why?

4.7

The passage is full of the kind of assertive statements for which Oscar Wilde was famous. For example:
Youth is the one thing worth having.

Beauty is the wonder of wonders.
Time is jealous of you.

Do you think they are true or superficial? Find some more, and try to explain how they relate to the idea of Dorian's happiness.

4.8 _____

What kind of happiness is this passage about? How does it compare with the happiness in the other texts you have read?

Discussion

There are a lot of expressions in English connected with happiness. Consider some of the following and discuss what you think they mean. Are there similar expressions in your own language?

to be as happy as a lark
to strike a happy medium
to be tickled pink
to be on cloud nine
to be on top of the world
to be in seventh heaven
to walk on air
to be over the moon

5 ▣

The moral of the previous story could be 'seize the day' – enjoy yourself while you can. Now we find a couple who are approaching marriage, and planning their future together with no illusions and no romantic dreams! Millamant explains . . .

from THE WAY OF THE WORLD

Millamant My dear Liberty, shall I leave thee? My faithful Solitude, my darling Contemplation, must I bid you then adieu? Ay-h adieu! My Morning Thoughts, agreeable Wakings, indolent Slumbers, adieu! – I can't do it! 'Tis more than
5 impossible! – Positively, Mirabell, I'll lie a-bed in a morning as long as I please.
Mirabell Then I'll get up in a morning as early as I please.
Millamant Ah! Idle creature, get up when you will! And, d'ye

hear, I won't be called names after I'm married. Positively, I
10   won't be called names.

Mirabell Names!

Millamant Aye. As wife, spouse, my dear, joy, jewel, love,
sweetheart, and the rest of that nauseous cant, in which men
and their wives are so fulsomely familiar. I shall never bear
15   that. Good Mirabell, don't let us be familiar or fond, nor kiss
before folks, like my Lady Fadler and Sir Francis; nor go to
Hyde Park together the first Sunday in a new chariot to
provoke eyes and whispers, and then never be seen there
together again; as if we were proud of one another the first
20   week, and ashamed of one another ever after. Let us never
visit together, nor go to a play together, but let us be very
strange and well bred. Let us be as strange as if we have been
married a great while, and as well bred as if we were not
married at all.

25   *Mirabell* Have you any more conditions to offer? Hitherto your
demands are pretty reasonable.

Millamant Trifles. As liberty to pay and receive visits to and
from whom I please; to write and receive letters without
interrogatories or wry faces on your part; to wear what I
30   please, and choose conversation with regard only to my
own taste; to have no obligation upon me to converse with wits
that I don't like, because they are your acquaintance, or to be
intimate with fools because they may be your relations; come
to dinner when I please, dine in my dressing-room when I'm
35   out of humour, without giving a reason; to have my closet
inviolate; to be sole empress of my tea table, which you must
never presume to approach without first asking leave; and
lastly, where-ever I am, you shall always knock at the door
before you come in. These articles subscribed, if I continue to
40   endure you a little longer, I may by degrees dwindle into a
wife.

William Congreve

5.1

What do you think of Mirabell's replies? Do they make him seem weak,
stupid, or intelligent?

5.2

What kind of list of necessary things would you make before
committing yourself to such a relationship as marriage? Do women and
men have different requests?

5.3

Do you think Mirabell and Millamant love each other? How important
is love to the pleasures of a relationship, in your opinion?

5.4

Can you tell anything about the kind of society these two lovers live in?
Do you think the conversation is serious or comic? How can you tell?

5.5

Find words or phrases in the passage which have the following equivalents:

you	until now
say goodbye to you	small things
lazy sleep	questions
in bed	complaining looks
such as/like	people who think they are funny
disgusting hypocritical talk	bedroom
exaggeratedly	the only dominating personality
loving	permission
people	conditions agreed
civilized, dignified	slowly decline

Graffiti

Not all that tempts your wand'ring eyes
And heedless hearts is lawful prize;
Nor all that glisters gold.

Thomas Gray

Happiness is a how, not a what; a talent, not an object.

Hermann Hesse

Happiness: an agreeable sensation arising from contemplating the misery of another.

Ambrose Bierce

A thing of beauty is a joy forever.

John Keats

Tasks

1 In two or three short paragraphs, discuss the meaning of happiness for the speakers of the texts in this chapter.
2 Write a short poem, a letter or an aphorism where your idea of happiness is expressed in a few words.

EDUCATION

What is the meaning of education, Sandy?

Some people say schooldays are 'the happiest days of your life'. Others disagree!

What's your opinion?
Are there things you enjoy learning? What makes them enjoyable – your own interest, the subject, the teacher, companions, or what?

1 📼

Music can be one of the most satisfying things to learn – but also one of the most difficult. If you can play an instrument, or are trying to learn, tell the group about some of the difficulties (and satisfactions) involved.
Alastair Reid, in this poem, advises a child playing the piano to 'try to be nobody, nothing'. Listen to the poem twice, reading the first time, and not reading, being 'nobody', the second time. See if you can 'feel what is happening strangely' as you hear the poem again.

TO A CHILD AT THE PIANO

Play the tune again; but this time
with more regard for the movement at the source of it,
and less attention to time. Time falls
curiously in the course of it.

5 Play the tune again; not watching
your fingering, but forgetting, letting flow
the sound till it surrounds you. Do not count
or even think. Let go.

Play the tune again; but try to be
10 nobody, nothing, as though the pace
of the sound were your heart beating, as though
the music were your face.

Play the tune again. It should be easier
to think less every time of the notes, of the measure.
15 It is all an arrangement of silence. Be silent, and then
play it for your pleasure.

Play the tune again; and this time, when it ends,
do not ask me what I think. Feel what is happening
strangely in the room as the sound glooms over
20 you, me, everything.

Now,
play the tune again.

Alastair Reid

1.1

Look at the list below of things we must not do if we are to follow the recommendations of the speaker/poet. On the right, list what we should do instead:

pay less attention to time ....

do not watch your fingering ....

do not count ....

think less of the notes ....

do not ask what I think ....

1.2

Even if you do not play an instrument, you probably often enjoy music. What kind of music do you enjoy, and why? Does your enjoyment come from the sound, or is there more to it than that? Does knowing the 'notes' help towards responding to music better?

1.3

The words 'play the tune again' appear five times, with different instructions each time, and a sixth time as a final invitation implying that it should be possible, 'now', for the child to get all the potential out of the tune. If the words were 'read the poem again', what other changes would have to be made? Would the message be very different?

1.4

Can you explain the following words and expressions in your own words:

time (line 1)
time (line 3)
Time falls curiously (lines 3 – 4)
letting flow the sound (lines 6 – 7)
the pace of the sound (lines 10 – 11)
as though the music were your face (lines 11 – 12)
as the sound glooms (line 19)

1.5

How much silence can you find in the text? Look for pauses in the poem, and for anything connected with the idea of silence.
Do you think silence is important in music? And in poetry?

1.6

How much does this poem have to do with 'learning'? Is it just about the piano, in your opinion, or could there be more to it than that?

2 📼

from THE PRIME OF MISS JEAN BRODIE

Miss Brodie is a schoolteacher in her prime (at least she thinks so) with very clear ideas on education. As you read and listen to the passage, decide if she sounds like the kind of teacher you would like, and who Miss Mackay is.

Their walk had brought them into broad Chambers Street. The group had changed its order, and was now walking three abreast, with Miss Brodie in front between Sandy and Rose. "I am summoned to see the headmistress at morning break on
5 Monday," said Miss Brodie. "I have no doubt Miss Mackay wishes to question my methods of instruction. It has happened before. It will happen again. Meanwhile, I follow my principles of education and give of my best in my prime. The word 'education' comes from the root *e* from *ex,* out, and *duco,* I lead. It means a
10 leading out. To me education is a leading out of what is already there in the pupil's soul. To Miss Mackay it is a putting in of something that is not there, and that is not what I call education, I call it intrusion, from the Latin root prefix *in* meaning in and the stem *trudo,* I thrust. Miss Mackay's method is to thrust a lot of
15 information into the pupil's head; mine is a leading out of knowledge, and that is true education as is proved by the root meaning. Now Miss Mackay has accused me of putting ideas into my girls' heads, but in fact that is *her* practice and mine is quite the opposite. Never let it be said that I put ideas into your
20 heads. What is the meaning of education, Sandy?"

Muriel Spark

2.1

Who do 'their' and 'them' in line 1 refer to ?

2.2

'Three abreast' (line 2) should give you an idea of the kind of group Miss Brodie leads. Who is she talking to in lines 3 – 20?

2.3

What sort of relationship is there between Miss Brodie and Miss Mackay ? What is Miss Brodie's attitude to the questioning she foresees for Monday morning? Choose from the following adjectives, giving reasons for your choice:

fatalistic	accepting
self-pitying	resigned
complacent	self-satisfied
triumphant	embittered
submissive	detached
aggressive	threatening
indifferent	

2.4

The last sentence is, in some way, the author's comment on what Miss Brodie has been saying. Can you say whether it sounds approving, disapproving, ironical, humorous, or anything else?

2.5 _____

'Putting ideas into my girls' heads' – has this only a negative connotation, or could it be a positive thing? Is there a difference between ideas and information? If so, what?

2.6 _____

How would you define Miss Brodie's attitude to her own method? Consider lines 14 – 17 in particular.

2.7 _____

Using your imagination and information in the passage, describe Miss Brodie (her physical appearance, her personality, etc.) then compare and discuss your portrait with that of others in the class.

3 ▣

Sometimes at school the relationship between teacher and pupils is a battle rather than a collaboration. As you read and listen to this passage, decide what the attitude of the pupils is to the new teacher, Paul, and who dominates in the end.

from DECLINE AND FALL

"That's your little mob in there," said Grimes; "you let them out at eleven."

"But what am I to teach them?" said Paul in sudden panic.

"Oh, I shouldn't try to *teach* them anything, not just yet,
5 anyway. Just keep them quiet."

"Now that's a thing I've never learned to do, " sighed Mr Prendergast.

Paul watched him amble into his classroom at the end of the passage, where a burst of applause greeted his arrival. Dumb
10 with terror he went into his own classroom.

Ten boys sat before him, their hands folded, their eyes bright with expectation.

"Good morning, sir," said the one nearest him.

"Good morning," said Paul.
15 "Good morning, sir," said the next.

"Good morning," said Paul.

"Good morning, sir," said the next.

"Oh shut up," said Paul.

At this the boy took out a handkerchief and began to cry
20 quietly.

"Oh, sir," came a chorus of reproach, "you've hurt his feelings. He's very sensitive; it's his Welsh blood, you know; it makes people very emotional. Say 'Good morning' to him sir, or he won't be happy all day. After all, it is a good morning, isn't it, sir?"
25 "Silence!" shouted Paul above the uproar, and for a few moments things were quieter.

"Please, sir," said a small voice – Paul turned and saw a grave-looking youth holding up his hand – "please, sir, perhaps he's been smoking cigars and doesn't feel well."
30 "Silence!" said Paul again.

The ten boys stopped talking and sat perfectly still staring at him. He felt himself getting hot and red under their scrutiny.

"I suppose the first thing I ought to do is to get your names clear. What is your name?" he asked, turning to the first boy.

35   "Tangent, sir."

"And yours?"

"Tangent, sir," said the next boy. Paul's heart sank.

"But you can't both be called Tangent."

"No, sir, *I'm* Tangent. He's just trying to be funny."

40   "I like that. *Me* trying to be funny! Please sir, I'm Tangent, sir; really I am."

"If it comes to that," said Clutterbuck from the back of the room, "there is only one Tangent here, and that is me. Anyone else can jolly well go to blazes."

45   Paul felt desperate.

"Well, is there anyone who isn't Tangent?"

Four or five voices instantly arose.

"I'm not, sir; I'm not Tangent. I wouldn't be called Tangent, not on the end of a barge pole."

50   In a few seconds the room had become divided into two parties: those who were Tangent and those were not. Blows were already being exchanged, when the door opened and Grimes came in. There was a slight hush.

"I thought you might want this," he said, handing Paul a

55 walking-stick. "And if you take my advice, you'll set them something to do."

He went out; and Paul, firmly grasping the walking-stick, faced his form.

"Listen," he said. "I don't care a damn what any of you are

60 called, but if there's another word from anyone I shall keep you all in this afternoon."

"You can't keep me in," said Clutterbuck; "I'm going for a walk with Captain Grimes."

"Then I shall very nearly kill you with this stick. Meanwhile you

65 will all write an essay on 'Self-indulgence'. There will be a prize of half a crown for the longest essay, irrespective of any possible merit."

From then onwards all was silence until break. Paul, still holding his stick, gazed despondently out of the window. Now

70 and then there rose from below the shrill voices of the servants scolding each other in Welsh. By the time the bell rang Clutterbuck had covered sixteen pages, and was awarded the half-crown.

"Did you find those boys difficult to manage?" asked Mr

75 Prendergast, filling his pipe.

"Not at all," said Paul.

Evelyn Waugh

3.1 _____

Decide which of the following best describes the pupils' attitude to Paul and support your reasons with quotations from the text.

a They want to make fun of him.

b They want to humiliate him.

c They are studying him.

d They want to extort half a crown.

e They want to be dominated by him.

f They feel hostile towards him.
g They want to prove their power over him.

3.2

When Paul answers that he did not find it at all difficult to manage the boys, do you think he is telling the truth?

3.3

Why do you think 'there was a slight hush' when Grimes came in? Do the boys fear him or respect him, or neither of these?

3.4

What contrasts can you find between Grimes's attitude, Mr Prendergast's and Paul's?

3.5

Do you think the pupils learn a lot in this kind of school? What is your opinion of lengthy essays winning prizes 'irrespective of any possible merit'?

3.6

There is a lot of colloquial language in this text. Here are some of the words and phrases you might need to check in the dictionary. Discuss with the rest of the class which expressions are most obvious, and which are not so clear to you.

can jolly well go to blazes	little mob
not on the end of a barge pole	sudden panic
if it comes to that	amble
uproar	dumb with terror
scrutiny	shouted
I thought you might want this	hot and red
you'll set them something to do	Paul's heart sank
you will all write an essay	despondently
blows were already being exchanged	

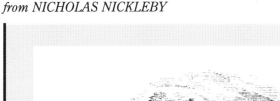

from NICHOLAS NICKLEBY

Now another example of a school scene, this time from Charles Dickens's *Nicholas Nickleby.* Mr Squeers, the headmaster of Dotheboys Hall, demonstrates his philosophy of education to Nicholas, his new assistant. Try to decide what Nicholas's feelings are about Squeers.

He could not but observe how silent and sad the boys all seemed to be. There was none of the noise and clamour of a school-room, none of its boisterous play or hearty mirth. The children sat crouching and shivering together, and seemed to
5   lack the spirit to move about. The only pupil who evinced the slightest tendency towards locomotion or playfulness was Master Squeers, and as his chief amusement was to tread upon the other boys' toes in his new boots, his flow of spirits was rather disagreeable than otherwise.
10   After some half-hour's delay Mr Squeers reappeared, and the boys took their places and their books, of which latter commodity the average might be about one to eight learners. A few minutes having elapsed, during which Mr Squeers looked very profound, as if he had a perfect apprehension of what was
15   inside all the books, and could say every word of their contents by heart if he only chose to take the trouble, that gentleman called up the first class.
Obedient to this summons, there ranged themselves in front of the schoolmaster's desk, half a dozen scarecrows, out at knees
20   and elbows, one of whom placed a torn and filthy book beneath his learned eye.
"This is the first class in English spelling and philosophy, Nickleby," said Squeers, beckoning Nicholas to stand beside him. "We'll get up a Latin one, and hand that over to you. Now,

25 then, where's the first boy?"

"Please, sir, he's cleaning the back parlour window," said the temporary head of the philosophical class.

"So he is, to be sure," rejoined Squeers. "We go upon the practical mode of teaching, Nickleby; the regular education
30 system. C-l-e-a-n, clean, verb active, to make bright, to scour. W-i-n, win, d-e-r, winder, a casement. When the boy knows this out of book, he goes and does it. It's just the same principle as the use of globes. Where's the second boy?"

"Please, sir, he's weeding the garden," replied a small voice.
35 "To be sure," said Squeers, by no means disconcerted. "So he is. B-o-t, bot, t-i-n, bottin, n-e-y, bottinney, noun substantive, a knowledge of plants, he goes and knows 'em. That's our system, Nickleby; what do you think of it?"

"It's a very useful one, at any rate," answered Nicholas
40 significantly.

"I believe you," rejoined Squeers, not remarking the emphasis of his usher.

"Third boy, what's a horse?"

"A beast, sir," replied the boy.
45 "So it is," said Squeers. "Ain't it, Nickleby?"

"I believe there is no doubt of that, sir" answered Nicholas.

"Of course there isn't," said Squeers. "A horse is a quadruped, and quadruped's Latin for beast, as everybody that's gone through the grammar knows, or else where's the use of having
50 grammars at all?"

"Where, indeed!" said Nicholas abstractedly.

"As you're perfect in that," resumed Squeers, turning to the boy, "go and look after *my* horse, and rub him down well, or I'll rub you down. The rest of the class go and draw water up till
55 somebody tells you to leave off, for it's washing-day to-morrow, and they want the coppers filled."

So saying he dismissed the first class to their experiments in practical philosophy, and eyed Nicholas with a look half cunning and half doubtful, as if he were not altogether certain what he
60 might think of him by this time.

"That's the way we do it, Nickleby," he said, after a long pause.

Nicholas shrugged his shoulders in a manner that was scarcely perceptible, and said he saw it was.

"And a very good way it is, too," said Squeers. "Now just take
65 those fourteen little boys and hear them some reading, because you know you must begin to be useful, and idling about here won't do."

Mr Squeers said this as if it had suddenly occurred to him, either that he must not say too much to his assistant, or that his
70 assistant did not say enough to him in praise of the establishment. The children were arranged in a semi-circle round the new master, and he was soon listening to their dull, drawling, hesitating recital of those stories of engrossing interest which are to be found in the more antiquated spelling
75 books.

In this exciting occupation the morning lagged heavily on.

Charles Dickens

4.1 _____

What are your reactions to Squeers's definitions and spellings?

4.2 _____

Which lines illustrate Mr Squeers's philosophy of education and his attitude to it? What are its advantages and disadvantages?

4.3 _____

How is this situation similar to the one in the previous text? How is it different?

4.4 _____

How would you describe the character Squeers? How does he compare with Miss Jean Brodie?

4.5 _____

This scene is portrayed through Nicholas's eyes. Does this mean you sympathize more with him and the boys than you did with Paul and his students? How do your reactions differ to the two stories?

4.6 _____

As in the previous text, there is a lot of interesting vocabulary, 'evinced' (line 5) instead of 'showed', for example. Often two words are put together to increase their effect, like 'crouching and shivering' (line 4). Pick out the words and phrases you find unusual or problematic, and see if you can guess their meaning before looking them up in the dictionary to check how correct you were.

Discussion

The 'richness' of vocabulary is what makes novels and stories more enjoyable than just simple 'words on the page'. A debate could be organized in which one side prefers simplicity and easy language, and the other prefers language rich with sounds and images. Don't all take the same side!

Is it difficult to find a good teacher? Discuss what makes the ideal teacher, and the ideal school – if they exist!

5 📼

LAST LESSON OF THE AFTERNOON

When will the bell ring, and end this weariness?
How long have they tugged the leash, and strained apart,
My pack of unruly hounds! I cannot start
Them again on a quarry of knowledge they hate to hunt,
5 I can haul them and urge them no more.

No longer now can I endure the brunt
Of the books that lie out on the desks; a full threescore
Of several insults of blotted pages, and scrawl
Of slovenly work that they have offered me.
10 I am sick, and what on earth is the good of it all?
What good to them or me, I cannot see!
                        So, shall I take
My last dear fuel of life to heap on my soul
And kindle my will to a flame that shall consume
15 Their dross of indifference; and take the toll
Of their insults in punishment? – I will not! –

I will not waste my soul and my strength for this.
What do I care for all that they do amiss!
What is the point of this teaching of mine, and of this
20 Learning of theirs? It all goes down the same abyss.

What does it matter to me, if they can write
A description of a dog, or if they can't?
What is the point? To us both, it is all my aunt!
And yet I'm supposed to care, with all my might.

25 I do not, and will not; they won't and they don't; and that's all!
I shall keep my strength for myself; they can keep theirs as well.
Why should we beat our heads against the wall
Of each other? I shall sit and wait for the bell.

D. H. Lawrence

5.1 ———————————————————————————

What are the pupils compared to in lines 2 and 3? Do they seem willing pupils? How can you tell?

5.2 ———————————————————————————

Do you agree with the sentiments expressed in lines 19 and 20? Why, or why not?

5.3 ———————————————————————————

What verb can be put into line 25?

5.4 ———————————————————————————

What words and phrases do you particularly like in this text? Can you say why?

The teacher can get tired of lessons too – as we see in this poem. As you read it, decide whose voice is speaking and who 'they' are.

5.5

Does the end of the poem confirm or deny the speaker's earlier words?

Graffiti

If he had only learnt a little less, how infinitely better he might have taught much more!

Charles Dickens

We receive three educations, one from our parents, one from our schoolmasters, and one from the world. The third contradicts all that the first two teach us.

Charles, Baron de Montesquieu

Experience is a good teacher, but she sends in terrific bills.

Minna Antrim

Education kills by degrees.

Anon

Tasks

1 Write a description of your ideal teacher. Then make a list of all the things a teacher shouldn't be or do.
2 Jot down ideas for a letter to a friend explaining why you want/do not want to be a teacher.

Yours are strange fancies

In which direction are the birds going?

What makes the drawing deceptive?

Why do you think the artist wanted to create this kind of optical illusion?

1 📟

The way we see things depends on who we are, what we expect, other people's reactions – in short, no two people see the same thing. For example, here are two voices of infants. As you read and listen, say briefly what the main difference is between the two 'views'.

INFANT JOY

> "I have no name:
> "I am but two days old,"
> What shall I call thee?
> "I happy am,
> 5 "Joy is my name."
> Sweet joy befall thee!
>
> Pretty joy!
> Sweet joy but two days old,
> Sweet joy I call thee:
> 10 Thou dost smile,
> I sing the while,
> Sweet joy befall thee!
>
> *William Blake*

INFANT SORROW

> My mother groan'd! my father wept.
> Into the dangerous world I leapt:
> Helpless, naked, piping loud:
> Like a fiend hid in a cloud.
>
> 5 Struggling in my father's hands,
> Striving against my swadling bands.
> Bound and weary I thought best
> To sulk upon my mother's breast.
>
> *William Blake*

1.1

Which poem do you find easier to follow? Pick out the words you think are important in making the message clear – even words you don't know.

1.2

What old or archaic words can you find? What are their modern equivalents? Do they make the poem any less significant, in your opinion?

1.3

In Infant Joy, who 'sings', and why?

1.4

Look up the words you are not sure of. Does this confirm they were important, or not? How?

1.5

Try to explain the last lines of each verse in your own words (two are the same, which makes it easier!). Do you think they sum up the lines before them in any way?

1.6

Is either poem a true representation of infancy? Why? Why not?

2 📼

from OF MICE AND MEN

Those were *Songs of Innocence and Experience*, as Blake himself called them. In the next text, from an American story, we can see another kind of 'innocence'. Lennie likes to play 'with soft things' – but he is a bit simple, and does not know his own strength. As you read and listen, what impression do you get of Lennie?

Curley's wife moved away from him a little. "I think you're nuts," she said.

"No I ain't," Lennie explained earnestly. "George says I ain't. I like to pet nice things with my finger, sof' things."

5 She was a little bit reassured. "Well, who don't?" she said. "Ever'body likes that. I like to feel silk an' velvet. Do you like to feel velvet?"

Lennie chuckled with pleasure. "You bet, by God," he cried happily. "An' I had some, too. A lady give me some, an' that lady

10 was – my own Aunt Clara. She gave it right to me – 'bout this big a piece. I wisht I had that velvet right now." A frown came over his face. "I lost it," he said. "I ain't seen it for a long time."

Curley's wife laughed at him. "You're nuts," she said. "But you're a kinda nice fella. Jus' like a big baby. But a person can

15 see kinda what you mean. When I'm doin' my hair sometimes I jus' set an' stroke it 'cause it's so soft." To show how she did it, she ran her fingers over the top of her head. "Some people got kinda coarse hair," she said complacently. "Take Curley. His hair is jus' like wire. But mine is soft and fine. 'Course I brush it a lot.

20 That makes it fine. Here – feel right here." She took Lennie's hand and put it on her head. "Feel right aroun' there an' see how soft it is."

Lennie's big fingers fell to stroking her hair.

"Don't you muss it up," she said.

25 Lennie said, "Oh! That's nice," and he stroked harder. "Oh, that's nice."

"Look out, now, you'll muss it." And then she cried angrily,

"You stop it now, you'll mess it all up." She jerked her head sideways, and Lennie's finger closed on her hair and hung on.
30 "Let go," she cried. "You let go!"

Lennie was in a panic. His face was contorted. She screamed then, and Lennie's other hand closed over her mouth and nose. "Please don't," he begged. "Oh! Please don't do that. George'll be mad."
35 She struggled violently under his hands. Her feet battered on the hay and she writhed to be free; and from under Lennie's hand came a muffled screaming. Lennie began to cry with fright. "Oh! Please don't do none of that," he begged. "George gonna say I done a bad thing. He ain't gonna let me tend no rabbits." He
40 moved his hand a little and her hoarse cry came out. Then Lennie grew angry. "Now don't ," he said. "I don't want you to yell. You gonna get me in trouble jus' like George says you will. Now don't you do that." And she continued to struggle, and her eyes were wild with terror. He shook her then, and he was angry
45 with her. "Don't you go yellin'," he said, and he shook her; and her body flopped like a fish. And then she was still, for Lennie had broken her neck.

He looked down at her, and carefully he removed his hand from over her mouth, and she lay still. "I don't want ta hurt you," he
50 said, "but George'll be mad if you yell." When she didn't answer nor move he bent closely over her. He lifted her arm and let it drop. For a moment he seemed bewildered. And then he whispered in fright, "I done a bad thing. I done another bad thing."

John Steinbeck

2.1
What is Curley's wife's impression of Lennie?

2.2
Pick out moments when Lennie is happy. When does this happiness change?

2.3
Why do you think Lennie is afraid of what George will say?

2.4
Does Lennie mean to kill Curley's wife? Why does it happen?

2.5
Try to tell the story again very briefly in your own words.

2.6
Listen to and read the story again, then discuss with the class:
– what Lennie thinks of himself
– what Curley's wife thinks of him
– what George will think of him
– what you think of him

3

from THE BLACK CAT

The next story is a case of seeing – and not seeing! The black cat of the title is the instrument of conscience. As you read, find out how the murderer's guilty secret is revealed.

One day she accompanied me upon some house-hold errand into the cellar of the old building which our poverty compelled us to inhabit. The cat followed me down the steep stairs, and nearly throwing me headlong, exasperated me to madness. Uplifting an
5 axe and forgetting in my wrath the childish dread which had hitherto stayed my hand, I aimed a blow at the animal, which of course would have proved instantly fatal had it descended as I wished. But this blow was arrested by the hand of my wife. Goaded by the interference into a rage more than demoniacal, I
10 withdrew my arm from her grasp and buried the axe in her brain. She fell dead upon the spot without a groan.

This hideous murder accomplished, I set myself forthwith and with entire deliberation to the task of concealing the body. I knew that I could not remove it from the house, either by day or
15 by night, without the risk of being observed by the neighbours. Many projects entered my mind. At one period I thought of cutting the corpse into minute fragments and destroying them by fire. At another I resolved to dig a grave for it in the floor of the cellar. Again, I deliberated about casting it in the well in the yard
20 – about packing it in a box, as if merchandise, with the usual arrangements, and so getting a porter to take it from the house. Finally, I hit upon what I considered a far better expedient than either of these. I determined to wall it up in the cellar – as the monks of the middle ages are recorded to have walled up their
25 victims.

For a purpose such as this the cellar was well adapted. Its walls were loosely constructed and had lately been plastered throughout with a rough plaster, which the dampness of the atmosphere had prevented from hardening. Moreover, in one of
30 the walls was a projection caused by a false chimney or fireplace, that had been filled up and made to resemble the rest of the

cellar. I made no doubt that I could readily displace the bricks at this point, insert the corpse, and wall the whole up as before, so that no eye could detect anything suspicious.

35 And in this calculation I was not deceived. By means of a crow-bar I easily dislodged the bricks, and having carefully deposited the body against the inner wall, I propped it in that position, while with little trouble I re-laid the whole structure as it originally stood. Having procured mortar, sand, and hair with

40 every possible precaution, I prepared a plaster which could not be distinguished from the old, and with this I very carefully went over the new brick-work. When I had finished I felt satisfied that all was right. The wall did not present the slightest appearance of having been disturbed. The rubbish on the floor was picked up

45 with the minutest care. I looked around triumphantly, and said to myself – "Here at last, then, my labour has not been in vain".

My next step was to look for the beast which had been the cause of so much wretchedness, for I had at length firmly resolved to put it to death. Had I been able to meet with it at the

50 moment there could have been no doubt of its fate, but it appeared that the crafty animal had been alarmed at the violence of my previous anger, and forebore to present itself in my present mood. It is impossible to describe or to imagine the deep, the blissful sense of relief which the absence of the

55 detested creature occasioned in my bosom. It did not make its appearance during the night – and thus for one night at least since its introduction into the house I suddenly and tranquilly slept; aye, slept even with the burden of murder upon my soul!

The second and the third day passed, and still my tormentor

60 came not. Once again I breathed as a free man. The monster, in terror, had fled the premises for ever! I should behold it no more! My happiness was supreme! The guilt of my dark deed disturbed me but little. Some few inquiries had been made, but these had been readily answered. Even a search had been instituted – but

65 of course nothing was to be discovered. I looked upon my future felicity as secured.

Upon the fourth day of the assassination, a party of the police came very unexpectedly into the house, and proceeded again to make rigorous investigation of the premises. Secure, however, in

70 the inscrutability of my place of concealment, I felt no embarrassment whatever. The officers bade me accompany them in their search. They left no nook or corner unexplored. At length, for the third or fourth time, they descended into the cellar. I quivered not in a muscle. My heart beat calmly as that of

75 one who slumbers in innocence. I walked the cellar from end to end. I folded my arms upon my bosom, and roamed easily to and fro. The police were thoroughly satisfied and prepared to depart. The glee at my heart was too strong to be restrained. I burned to say if but one word by way of triumph, and to render doubly sure

80 their assurance of my guiltlessness.

"Gentlemen," I said at last, as the party ascended the steps, "I delight to have allayed your suspicions. I wish you all health, and a little more courtesy. By-the-by, gentlemen, this – this is a very well constructed house." [In the rabid desire to say something

85 easily, I scarcely knew what I uttered at all.] "I may say an *excellently* well-constructed house. These walls – are you going, gentlemen? – these walls are solidly put together;" and here, through the mere frenzy of bravado, I rapped heavily with a cane which I held in my hand upon that very portion of the brick-work
90 behind which stood the corpse of the wife of my bosom.

But may God shield and deliver me from the fangs of the arch-fiend! No sooner had the reverberation of my blows sunk into silence than I was answered by a voice from within the tomb! – by a cry, at first muffled and broken, like the sobbing of a child,
95 and then quickly swelling into one long, loud, and continuous scream, utterly anomalous and inhuman – a howl – a wailing shriek, half of horror and half of triumph, such as might have arisen only out of hell, conjointly from the throats of the damned in their agony and of the demons that exult in the damnation.
100 Of my own thoughts it is folly to speak. Swooning, I staggered to the opposite wall. For one instant the party upon the stairs remained motionless, through extremity of terror and of awe. In the next a dozen stout arms were toiling at the wall. It fell bodily. The corpse already greatly decayed and clotted with gore, stood
105 erect before the eyes of the spectators. Upon its head, with red extended mouth and solitary eye of fire, sat the hideous beast whose craft had seduced me into murder, and whose informing voice had consigned me to the hangman. I had walled the monster up within the tomb!

Edgar Allan Poe

3.1

Look at the story paragraph by paragraph.

1st Who is 'she' (line 1)? What does the cat do? Why does the speaker kill his wife?

2nd How many ways of disposing of the body does he think of? Which does he finally choose?

3rd and *4th* Is it easy for him to hide the body? Explain why or why not.

5th and *6th* Why does he want to find the cat? How does the murderer now feel?

7th and *8th* How does he show his confidence during the police search?

9th and *10th* What has happened?

3.2

What can you conclude about:
a the narrator?
b the cat?
c the general atmosphere of the story?

3.3

Who do you feel sympathy for (if anyone!)?

3.4

What was it that 'consigned' the narrator 'to the hangman': the cat's voice, or his own will for self-punishment? Discuss this with others in the class, then summarize the extract, adding your comments.

4 ▦

The next text shows how a Martian sees our familiar world – but, of course, to him or her, it is not at all familiar! As you read and listen, what elements of the real world can you recognize?

A MARTIAN SENDS A POSTCARD HOME

Caxtons are mechanical birds with many wings
and some are treasured for their markings –

they cause the eyes to melt
or the body to shriek without pain.

5   I have never seen one fly, but
sometimes they perch on the hand.

Mist is when the sky is tired of flight
and rests its soft machine on ground:

then the world is dim and bookish
10 like engravings under tissue paper.

Rain is when the earth is television.
It has the property of making colours darker.

Model T is a room with the lock inside –
a key is turned to free the world

15 for movement, so quick there is a film
to watch for anything missed.

But time is tied to the wrist
or kept in a box, ticking with impatience.

In homes, a haunted apparatus sleeps,
20 that snores when you pick it up.

If the ghost cries, they carry it
to their lips and soothe it to sleep

with sounds. And yet, they wake it up
deliberately, by tickling with a finger.

25 Only the young are allowed to suffer
openly. Adults go to a punishment room

with water but nothing to eat.
They lock the door and suffer the noises

alone. No one is exempt
30 and everyone's pain has a different smell.

At night, when all the colours die,
they hide in pairs

and read about themselves –
in colour, with their eyelids shut.

Craig Raine

4.1

Caxton was the first English printer of books, and the Model T the first mass-produced Ford car. Can you identify some other more familiar items?

4.2

The descriptions of rain and a watch are probably the clearest. Pick them out, and discuss how they seem to you.

4.3

The bathroom and sleeping seem unusual to the Martian. How do you react to the descriptions? Did you find them funny?

4.4

What do you think the 'haunted apparatus' (line 19) is?

4.5

Which words surprise you most? Are there any descriptions you find difficult to understand? Does this reflect the Martian's difficulty in understanding what he/she sees?

4.6

Discuss how appropriate the Martian's descriptions are. Can you think of other things you could describe in this defamiliarized way?

4.7

What do you think of the title? Try writing some Martian postcards of your own.

Discussion

Discuss with the class how we can judge and be judged: appearances, behaviour, expectations, preconceptions, fears and insecurities, familiarity and unfamiliarity are all involved in this. Refer back to the texts in this chapter for examples during the discussion.

5

All the texts we have read in this chapter have shown us different points of view or perspectives: positive contrasted with negative, gentle with strong, innocent with guilty, and so on. Now we have a story about literally seeing something attractive, finding it, and looking back at the starting-point of the journey. As you read, see how much you think is real, and how much is the 'rainbow's end, in fairy land.'

from THE PIAZZA

From the piazza, some uncertain object I had caught, mysteriously snugged away, to all appearance, in a sort of purpled breast-pocket, high up in a hopper-like hollow, or sunken angle, among the north-western mountains –

5 Indeed, for a year or more, I knew not there was such a spot, and might, perhaps, have never known, had it not been for a wizard afternoon in autumn – late in autumn – a mad poet's afternoon; the hermit-sun did little else but just steadily paint one small, round, strawberry mole upon the wan cheek of north-

10 western hills. Signal as a candle. One spot of radiance, where all else was shade.

Fairies there, thought I; some haunted ring where fairies dance.

Time passed; and the following May, after a gentle shower upon the mountains, I saw a rainbow, resting its further end just

15 where, in autumn, I had marked the mole. Fairies there, thought I; remembering that rainbows bring out the blooms, and that, if one can but get to the rainbow's end, his fortune is made in a bag of gold. Yon rainbow's end, would I were there, thought I. Whatever it was, viewed through the rainbow's medium, it

20 glowed like the Potosi mine.

I was sitting out, in the September morning, upon the piazza when, suddenly looking off, I saw the golden mountain-window, dazzling like a deep-sea dolphin. Fairies there, thought I, once more; the queen of fairies at her fairy window; at any rate, some

25 glad mountain-girl; it will do me good, it will cure this weariness, to look on her. No more; I'll launch my yawl – ho, cheerly, heart! and push away for fairy-land – for rainbow's end, in fairy-land.

How to get to fairy-land, by what road, I did not know; nor could any one inform me; not even one, Edmund Spenser, who had

30 been there. I took the fairy-mountain's bearings, and the first fine day away I sailed, free voyager as an autumn leaf. Early dawn; and, sallying westward, I sowed the morning before me.

After miles of horse-riding through pastures and deep woods, of walking along rivers and rapids and through brakes "that tried to

35 put me back", of climbing up "slippery steeps", "foot-sore and weary" I finally got there.

Fairy-land at last, thought I; Una and her lamb dwell here. Truly, a small abode – mere palanquin, set down on the summit, in a pass between two worlds, participant of neither.

40 Pausing at the threshold, or rather where threshold once had been, I saw, through the open door-way, a lonely girl, sewing at a lonely window. A pale-cheeked girl, and fly-specked window, with wasps about the mended upper panes. I spoke. She shyly started. Recovering, she bade me enter; with her apron brushed off a

45 stool; then silently resumed her own. With thanks I took the stool; but now, for a space, I, too, was mute. This, then, is the fairy-mountain house, and here, the fairy queen sitting at her fairy window.

I went up to it. Downwards, directed by the tunneled pass, as

50 through a leveled telescope, I caught sight of a far-off, soft, azure

world. I hardly knew it, though I came from it.

"You must find this view very pleasant," said I, at last.

"Oh, sir," tears starting in her eyes, "the first time I looked out of this window, I said 'never, never shall I weary of this' ".

55 "And what wearies you of it now?"

"I don't know," while a tear fell; "but it is not the view, it is Marianna."

Silent I stood by the fairy window, while these things were being told.

60 "Do you know," she said at last, as stealing from her story, "do you know who lives yonder? – I have never been down into that country – away off there, I mean; that house, that marble one," pointing far across the lower landscape; "have you not caught it? there, on the long hill-side: the field before, the woods behind;

65 the white shines out against their blue; don't you mark it? the only house in sight."

I looked; and after a time, to my surprise, recognized, more by its position than its aspect, or Marianna's description, my own abode, glimmering much like this mountain one from the piazza.

70 The mirage haze made it appear less a farm-house than King Charming's palace.

"I have often wondered who lives there; but it must be some happy one; again this morning was I thinking so."

"Some happy one," returned I, starting; "and why do you think

75 that? You judge some rich one lives there?"

"Rich or not, I never thought; but it looks so happy, I can't tell how; and it is so far away. Sometimes I think I do but dream it is there. You should see it in a sunset."

"No doubt the sunset gilds it finely; but not more than the

80 sunrise does this house, perhaps."

"This house? The sun is a good sun, but it never gilds this house. Why should it? This old house is rotting."

"Yours are strange fancies, Marianna."

"They but reflect the things."

85 "Then I should have said, 'These are strange things,' rather than, 'Yours are strange fancies.' "

"As you will"; and took up her sewing.

Herman Melville

5.1 ――――――――――――――――――――――――――――――――――

What did the narrator see from the piazza, in your opinion? And what did it turn out to be?

5.2 ――――――――――――――――――――――――――――――――――

What did Marianna see when she looked towards the piazza?

5.3 ――――――――――――――――――――――――――――――――――

Can you find images of the sea, travelling and mythology?
What, if anything, do you think they add to the basic story-line?

5.4

Using only the context as you understand it, try to substitute the following words and phrases from the text with simpler words you know.

snugged (line 2)	sallying (line 32)
hopper-like hollow (line 3)	brakes (line 34)
mole (lines 9 and 15)	dwell (line 37)
wan (line 9)	palanquin (line 38)
launch my yawl (line 26)	gilds (lines 79 and 81)
ho, cheerly, heart! (line 26)	As you will (line 87)

5.5

There are lots of exophoric references – that is, references to things outside the text, or quotations from other texts. 'The Potosi mine' (line 20) and 'Edmund Spenser' (line 29) are two of these. Do they add anything to your understanding, or do they get in the way – or are they not important to your understanding of the whole story? Find some more, and discuss their effectiveness, or how effective the story would be without them.

5.6

There are several fairy elements in the fable, represented by expressions like 'a wizard afternoon in autumn' (line 7), 'a mad poet's afternoon' (line 7), 'the hermit-sun' (line 8), 'some haunted ring where fairies dance' (line 12). Can you find any more?

5.7

Make an edited, single-paragraph version of the story, in the first person, then, in the third person. Compare your version with other students' and evaluate what has been left out, and why.

5.8

Some readers like to interpret this story in a symbolic way – do you agree that this is possible? Do you like such a reading? Why/why not?

Graffiti

Two men look out through the same bars:
One sees the mud, and one the stars.
Frederick Langbridge

Every truth has two faces, every rule two surfaces, every precept two applications.
General Joubert

Tasks

1 Make notes for each text in the chapter, identifying main ideas and points of view.
2 Choose the text you liked best and discuss the reasons why it appealed to you.

*Was it for this the clay
grew tall?*

Is there such a thing as 'nothing'?
What can it be?

Nothing, however it be multiplied,
will forever be nothing.

Thomas Hobbes

Nothing will come of nothing.

William Shakespeare

Absence makes the heart grow
fonder.

Traditional saying

What is the opposite of nothing, in
your opinion?
Is this kind of discussion futile?
Why or why not?

1 🖭

All the texts in this chapter are
concerned with something that
isn't the case, or that won't
happen: absence can be just as
significant as presence. As you
read and listen to this short lyric,
decide what the speaker will miss.

SO WE'LL GO NO MORE A-ROVING

So, we'll go no more a-roving
So late into the night,
Though the heart be still as loving
And the moon be still as bright.

5 For the sword outwears its sheath,
And the soul wears out the breast,
And the heart must pause to breathe,
And love itself have rest.

Though night was made for loving,
10 And the day returns too soon,
Yet we'll go no more a-roving
By the light of the moon.

Lord Byron

CHAPTER 5

1.1 _____

How do the first and last verses resemble each other? How is the
second verse different?

1.2 _____

What does the first word make you think of?

1.3 _____

Which line sums up the poem for you?

1.4 _____

Is it happy or sad, positive or negative, as you see it?

2 📼 _____

The next text was written during
war-time, the First World War
(1914 – 1918). A young soldier is
dying, and as the writer speaks
about him he reflects on the
futility of the situation. As you read
and listen, see if his reflections go
further.

FUTILITY

Move him into the sun –
Gently its touch awoke him once,
At home, whispering of fields unsown.
Always it woke him, even in France,
5 Until this morning and this snow.
If anything might rouse him now
The kind old sun will know.

Think how it wakes the seeds, –
Woke, once, the clays of a cold star.
10 Are limbs, so dear-achieved, are sides,
Full-nerved, – still warm, – too hard to stir?
Was it for this the clay grew tall?
– O what made fatuous sunbeams toil
To break earth's sleep at all?

Wilfred Owen

2.1 _____

What do the following words refer to?
him (lines 1,2,4,6)
its (line 2)
it (lines 4,8)
this (line 12)

2.2 _____

The poem is set in France. Pick out other references to place, and try to
work out what the dying man's job was before the war.

2.3

Now try and identify references to:

a time
b substance
c movement

2.4

What difference is there in the writer's attitude to the sun in lines 7 and 13?

2.5

Why are there so many references to waking?

2.6

Line 11 is a kind of climax: can you interpret what has happened to provoke the writer's question?

2.7

Is this poem without hope, or can you see anything positive in it?

2.8

The word 'fatuous' (13) means 'stupid, foolish, inane'. Can you see any connection between this and the title of the poem?

2.9

Is it an anti-war poem, in your opinion?

3

The next poem goes, perhaps, more deeply into the idea of personal loss – but emerges towards the end a little more positively. As you read and listen, try to find ideas of movement in the text.

NO. 341

> After great pain, a formal feeling comes –
> The Nerves sit ceremonious, like Tombs –
> The stiff Heart questions was it He, that bore,
> And Yesterday, or Centuries before?
>
> 5 The Feet, mechanical, go round –
> Of Ground, or Air, or Ought –
> A Wooden way
> Regardless grown,
> A Quartz contentment, like a stone –
>
> 10 This is the Hour of Lead –
> Remembered, if outlived,
> As Freezing persons, recollect the Snow –
> First – Chill – then Stupor – then the letting go –
>
> *Emily Dickinson*

3.1

Pick out phrases or single words that you notice in particular and compare yours with others in the group.

3.2 _____

Have you ever felt such 'pain'? Was it like this?

3.3 _____

What do you think lines 3 and 4 might mean?

3.4 _____

When does the heavy weight of the poem become lighter? Pick out images of weight, and discuss whether you find them clear.

3.5 _____

Do the dashes make the poem more effective, or would full stops be better?

3.6 _____

What title could you give to the poem?

---

4 _____

Querry, a famous architect, is being interviewed by a journalist, Parkinson, about his decision to give up his life in Europe and go to a leper colony in Africa. As you read, find out why he has wanted to escape, and how he feels now.

from A BURNT-OUT CASE

"No one has ever questioned your reputation."

"The future will. Somewhere in a back street of Brussels now there's a boy at a drawing-board who will show me up. I wish I could see the cathedral he will build... No, I don't. Or I wouldn't
5 be here. He'll be no spoilt priest. He'll pass the novice-master."

"I don't know what you are talking about, Querry. Sometimes you talk like Rycker."

"Do I? Perhaps he has the Masonic sign too..."

"If you are so bored, why not be bored in comfort? A little
10 apartment in Brussels or a villa in Capri. After all, you are a rich man, Querry."

"Boredom is worse in comfort. I thought perhaps out here there would be enough pain and enough fear to distract..." He looked at Parkinson. "Surely you can understand me if anyone can."
15 "I can't understand a word."

"Am I such a monster that even you...?"

"What about your work, Querry? Whatever you say, you can't be bored with that. You've been a raging success."

"You mean money? Haven't I told you that the work wasn't
20 good enough? What were any of my churches compared with the cathedral at Chartres? They were all signed with my name of course – nobody could mistake a Querry for a Corbusier, but which one of us knows the architect of Chartres? He didn't care. He worked with love not vanity – and with belief too, I suppose.
25 To build a church when you don't believe in a god seems a little indecent, doesn't it? When I discovered I was doing that, I accepted a commission for a city hall, but I didn't believe in politics either. You never saw such an absurd box of concrete and glass as I landed on the poor city square. You see I
30 discovered what seemed only to be a loose thread in my jacket –

I pulled it and all the jacket began to unwind. Perhaps it's true
that you can't believe in a god without loving a human being or
love a human being without believing in a god. They use the
phrase 'make love', don't they? But which of us are creative
35 enough to 'make' love? We can only be loved – if we are lucky."
    "Why are you telling me this, Mr Querry – even if it's true?"
    "Because at least you are someone who won't mind the truth,
though I doubt whether you'll ever write it. Perhaps – who
knows? – I might persuade you to drop altogether this absurd
40 pious nonsense that Rycker talks about me. I am no Schweitzer.
My God, he almost tempts me to seduce his wife. That at least
might change his tune."
    "Could you?"
    "It's an awful thing when experience and not vanity makes one
45 say yes."

Graham Greene

4.1

Where do you think the conversation takes place?

4.2

What are the points Querry is trying to make when he says that:

a the architect of Chartres 'didn't care' (line 23)?
b 'all the jacket began to unwind' (line 31)?

4.3

What do you think is Querry's attitude to:

a fame?
b wealth?
c love?
d Rycker?

4.4

Can you sympathize with Querry?

4.5

How important is the name of an architect, a designer or an artist who
'signs' his or her work?

4.6

This passage is really about rejection of values. Do you find it cynical or
realistic? Pick out phrases you find particularly significant to justify
your point of view.

4.7

Try to sum up Querry's problem in a few words.

Discussion

These last three texts require some emotional involvement on the part of the reader. Did they appeal to you emotionally? Is it necessary to have experienced similar things to the writer in order to fully appreciate these messages? What is the value of experience?

5 🔲

Hamlet, in the most famous soliloquy in English, tries to balance some of the negative elements we have seen with positive reasons for living. As you read and listen, find out if he finally decides 'to be', that is, to go on living, or 'not to be'. That is the question.

from HAMLET

> HAMLET. To be, or not to be, that is the question,
>   Whether 'tis nobler in the mind to suffer
>   The slings and arrows of outrageous fortune,
>   Or to take arms against a sea of troubles,
> 5   And by opposing, end them. To die, to sleep –
>   No more, and by a sleep to say we end
>   The heart-ache, and the thousand natural shocks
>   That flesh is heir to; 'tis a consummation
>   Devoutly to be wished. To die, to sleep;
> 10 To sleep, perchance to dream. Ay, there's the rub;
>   For in that sleep of death what dreams may come
>   When we have shuffled off this mortal coil
>   Must give us pause – there's the respect
>   That makes calamity of so long life:
> 15 For who would bear the whips and scorns of time,
>   Th'oppressor's wrong, the proud man's contumely,
>   The pangs of despis'd love, the law's delay,
>   The insolence of office, and the spurns
>   The patient merit of th'unworthy takes,
> 20 When he himself might his quietus make
>   With a bare bodkin; who would fardels bear,
>   To grunt and sweat under a weary life,
>   But that the dread of something after death,
>   The undiscovered country, from whose bourn
> 25 No traveller returns, puzzles the will,
>   And makes us rather bear those ills we have,
>   Than fly to others that we know not of?
>   Thus conscience does make cowards of us all,
>   And thus the native hue of resolution
> 30 Is sicklied o'er with the pale cast of thought,
>   And enterprises of great pitch and moment
>   With this regard their currents turn awry,
>   And lose the name of action.
>
> *William Shakespeare*

5.1 _____

Hamlet describes life and death in a variety of ways, using metaphors. Make a list of them, deciding which are positive, which negative. Do they seem effective to you as images, or do you find them artificial?

5.2

'Ay, there's the rub' (line 10) is a kind of turning-point, the phrase which changes the direction of the whole argument. Explain in your own words the list of troubles and problems that Hamlet then goes on to describe (lines 15 – 19). Are there more that you would like to add to the list?

5.3

Can you say in your own words why 'to dream' is such a problem?

5.4

Find words or phrases in the text which, in modern English, might have the following synonyms:

inherits	heavy loads
perhaps	boundary
left this human life	colour
disaster	importance
insolence	directions
final peace	in the wrong direction
little dagger	

Try substituting the modern words for the originals to make a 'new' reading of the speech. Does it work effectively? Which version do you prefer, and why?

5.5

What do you think is meant by 'conscience' (28)? Is living an act of cowardice or of courage, according to Hamlet? What do you think?

Graffiti

I think that nought is worth a thought,
And I'm a fool for thinking.

W. M. Praed

Tasks

1 Choose any of the texts in the chapter as a starting point to discuss some of the ideas that emerged in the analysis and discussion of its theme.
2 Change any of the texts into a different kind of text (a letter, a newspaper article, a telephone conversation, a diary entry, etc.) then exchange it with others in the class making sure they can relate it to the original.
3 Organize a debate or discussion on one or more of these notions.

   a We can only be loved – if we are lucky.
   b It's an awful thing when experience and not vanity makes one say 'yes'.
   c Boredom is worse in comfort.
   d If nothing has any meaning (as is the case for Querry), is there any point in living? What would you oppose to Querry's 'nothing'?
   e True values in modern society.

MONEY

Thou Being the Best of Things

Money makes the world go round.

Money is the root of all evil.

Do you agree that the love of money is the root of all evil?

MODERN PRAYER

> Almighty Mammon, make me rich!
> Make me rich quickly, with never a hitch
> in my fine prosperity! Kick those in the ditch
> who hinder me, Mammon, great son of a bitch!
>
> *D. H. Lawrence*

Do you think D.H. Lawrence's *Modern Prayer* is realistic – or is it a joke?

What attitude does 'kick those in the ditch who hinder me' reveal in the speaker?

Do the rhymes make the poem more effective, or less, in your opinion?

1 🖭

HOW PLEASANT IT IS TO HAVE MONEY from DIPSYCHUS

Probably most of us would like to have a lot of money – but how do you think you would behave if you were rich? Think of some of the things you would do; discuss them with a partner and with the rest of the class.

Now compare what you would do with what the speaker in the poem does. As you read and listen, decide if the speaker is really serious.

As I sat at the café I said to myself,
They may talk as they please about what they call pelf,
They may sneer as they like about eating and drinking,
But help it I cannot, I cannot help thinking,
5 How pleasant it is to have money, heigh ho!
How pleasant it is to have money.

I sit at my table *en grand seigneur*,
And when I have done, throw a crust to the poor;
Not only the pleasure, one's self, of good living,
10 But also the pleasure of now and then giving.
So pleasant it is to have money, heigh ho!
So pleasant it is to have money.

It was but last winter I came up to Town,
But already I'm getting a little renown;
15 I make new acquaintance where'er I appear.
I am not too shy, and have nothing to fear.
So pleasant it is to have money, heigh ho!
So pleasant it is to have money.

I drive through the streets, and I care not a damn;
20 The people they stare, and they ask who I am;
And if I should chance to run over a cad,
I can pay for the damage if ever so bad.
So pleasant it is to have money, heigh ho!
So pleasant it is to have money.

25 We stroll to our box and look down on the pit,
And if it weren't low should be tempted to spit;
We loll and we talk until people look up,
And when it's half over we go out and sup.
So pleasant it is to have money, heigh ho!
30 So pleasant it is to have money.

The best of the tables and best of the fare –
And as for the others, the devil may care;
It isn't our fault if they dare not afford
To sup like a prince and be drunk as a lord.
35 So pleasant it is to have money, heigh ho!
So pleasant it is to have money.

We sit at our tables and tipple champagne;
Ere one bottle goes, comes another again;
The waiters they skip and they scuttle about,
40 And the landlords attend us so civilly out.
So pleasant it is to have money, heigh ho!
So pleasant it is to have money.

Arthur Hugh Clough

1.1

Try to identify the various places the speaker visits, and what he does there.

1.2

Match the list of words from the poem with their dictionary definitions on the right. Then decide whether the connotations of the words used in the poem help the irony of the description, help to show the speaker's attitude better, or anything else.

pelf	drink
cad	run quickly
loll	vulgar person
sup	eat
tipple	money
scuttle	recline

1.3

What do you think these words and phrases mean: *en grand seigneur* (line 7), a crust to the poor (line 8), if ever so bad (line 22), be drunk as a lord (line 34)?

1.4

How would you describe the speaker's character?

1.5

What do they (line 2), we (line 25), it (line 26), it's (line 28) refer to?

1.6

How strongly does the poet feel about the manners of the rich? Where can you hear his voice?

1.7

What is the effect of:

a the rhyme?
b the rhythm?
c the refrain?

Can a light-hearted sing-song poem like this convey a serious message of social criticism? Discuss this with others in the class and make notes of the 'fors' and 'againsts'.

1.8

Who or what is the target of the poem?

2 ▣

Gordon Comstock, in a more
modern situation, presents the
opposite point of view – that of
someone who has no money. As
you read, pick out all the things
that lack of money denies him.

from KEEP THE ASPIDISTRA FLYING

Gordon gazed at the thing with wordless hatred. Perhaps no
snub in the world is so deadly as this, because none is so
unanswerable. Suddenly he loathed his own poem and was
acutely ashamed of it. He felt it the weakest, silliest poem ever
5 written. Without looking at it again he tore it into small bits and
flung them into the wastepaper basket. He would put that poem
out of his mind for ever. The rejection slip, however, he did not
tear up yet. He fingered it, feeling its loathly sleekness. Such an
elegant little thing, printed in admirable type. You could tell at a
10 glance that it came from a 'good' magazine – a snooty highbrow
magazine with the money of a publishing house behind it.
Money, money! Money and culture! It was a stupid thing that he
had done. Fancy sending a poem to a paper like the *Primrose*! As
though they'd accept poems from people like *him*. The mere fact
15 that the poem wasn't typed would tell them what kind of person
he was. He might as well have dropped a card on Buckingham
Palace. He thought of the people who wrote for the *Primrose*; a
coterie of moneyed highbrows – those sleek, refined young
animals who suck in money and culture with their mother's milk.
20 The idea of trying to horn in among that pansy crowd! But he
cursed them all the same. The sods! The bloody sods! "The
Editor regrets!" Why be so bloody mealy-mouthed about it? Why
not say outright, "We don't want your bloody poems. We only
take poems from chaps we were at Cambridge with. You
25 proletarians keep your distance?" The bloody, hypocritical sods!
At last he crumpled up the rejection slip, threw it away, and
stood up. Better get to bed while he had the energy to undress.
Bed was the only place that was warm. But wait. Wind the clock,
set the alarm. He went through the familiar action with a sense of
30 deadly staleness. His eye fell upon the aspidistra. Two years he
had inhabited this vile room; two mortal years in which nothing
had been accomplished. Seven hundred wasted days, all ending
in the lonely bed. Snubs, failures, insults, all of them unavenged.
Money, money, all is money! Because he had no money the
35 Dorings snubbed him, because he had no money the *Primrose*
had turned down his poem, because he had no money Rosemary
wouldn't sleep with him. Social failure, artistic failure, sexual
failure – they are all the same. And lack of money is at the
bottom of them all.

George Orwell

2.1 _____

What is the 'thing' in line 1? What does 'this' refer to in line 2? What
'stupid thing' had he done (line 12)?

2.2 _____

Find as many details as possible – inferred or real – of the setting where
the scene takes place.

2.3

Below, in jumbled order, are listed some adjectives related to Gordon's alternating moods in the passage. Arrange them in the sequence in which they follow each other in the text, writing down next to them the relevant quotations.

furious	wounded
self-mocking	angry
depressed	embittered
disgusted	filled with hatred
ashamed	

2.4

Some words in the text are particularly charged with emotions. Expand the ideas expressed by 'snooty', 'highbrow', 'coterie', 'pansy', 'mealy-mouthed'. Find one or two more examples.

2.5

How are 'money and culture' (line 12) associated in Gordon's mind? What is the cumulative effect of the repetition of this phrase (and others)?

2.6

Who says 'But wait' (line 28)? What other phrases are similar to this?

2.7

What differences do you notice between the first and second paragraphs? Compare the use of:

a verbs
b repetition
c movement
d unspoken thoughts

3 📼

How much money do you have? How much do you spend? This is a problem we all have. One of the most famous fictional bankrupts is Mr Micawber in Charles Dickens's *David Copperfield* – and he sums up his advice to young David in this passage. As you read and listen, see what contradiction you can find in Mr Micawber's words.

from DAVID COPPERFIELD

"My dear young friend," said Mr Micawber, "I am older than you; a man of some experience in life, and – and of some experience, in short, in difficulties, generally speaking. At present, and until something turns up (which I am, I may say,
5 hourly expecting), I have nothing to bestow but advice. Still my advice is so far worth taking, that – in short, that I have never taken it myself, and am the" – here Mr Micawber, who had been beaming and smiling, all over his head and face, up to the present moment, checked himself and frowned – "the miserable
10 wretch you behold."

"My dear Mr Micawber!" urged his wife.

"I say," returned Mr Micawber, quite forgetting himself, and smiling again, "the miserable wretch you behold. My advice is, never do tomorrow what you can do today. Procrastination is the
15 thief of time. Collar him!"

"My poor papa's maxim," Mrs Micawber observed.

"My dear," said Mr Micawber, "your papa was very well in his way, and Heaven forbid that I should disparage him. Take him for all in all, we ne'er shall – in short, make the acquaintance,
20 probably, of anybody else possessing, at his time of life, the same legs for gaiters, and able to read the same description of print, without spectacles. But he applied that maxim to our marriage, my dear; and that was so far prematurely entered into, in consequence, that I never recovered the expense."
25 Mr Micawber looked aside at Mrs Micawber, and added: "Not that I am sorry for it. Quite the contrary, my love." After which he was grave for a minute or so.

"My other piece of advice, Copperfield," said Mr Micawber, "you know. Annual income twenty pounds, annual expenditure
30 nineteen nineteen six, result happiness. Annual income twenty pounds, annual expenditure twenty pounds ought and six, result misery. The blossom is blighted, the leaf withered, the God of day goes down upon the dreary scene, and in short you are forever floored. As I am."

Charles Dickens

3.1 _____

What do you think Mr Micawber thinks of himself?

3.2 _____

There are only three short sentences of narratorial description in the passage. Do they give you a different insight into Mr Micawber?

3.3 _____

How do you think Mr Micawber regards his father-in-law? What good qualities does he recognize in him? Does he blame him for anything?

3.4 _____

Why do you think he hesitates and repeats himself? Locate all the signs of hesitation, and say what they contribute to the naturalness and authenticity of the conversation.

3.5 _____

What or who does the phrase "Collar him!" (line 15) refer to? What does it mean?

3.6 _____

The last three lines of the passage are unusually expressed in relation to the rest of Mr Micawber's words. What effects does he want to create?

4 _____

from RICEYMAN STEPS

Of course there are also people who have money but who don't want to spend it. This meanness, or miserliness, is often the subject of jokes – is this true in your country? Compare jokes and sayings about meanness; what aspects do they have in common? Sometimes in English a person is described as 'not mean, just careful'. Is this an appropriate description, in your opinion? In Arnold Bennett's novel of city life, *Riceyman Steps*, we have an example of someone who is perhaps 'mean', perhaps 'careful'; even on his wedding day Henry is watching how the money goes! As you read, see which words and phrases reflect Henry's preoccupation with money.

As Henry and Violet approached the turnstile, Henry murmured to Violet:

"How much is it? How much is it?"

"One and three, including tax," Violet murmured in reply.

5 Half a crown for the two was less than he had feared, but he felt in his trouser-pocket and half a crown was more than he had there, and he slowly pulled out of his breast-pocket an old Treasury-note case. The total expenses of the wedding ceremony at the Registry had been considerable; he seemed to have been

10 disbursing the whole time since they left Clerkenwell for the marriage and honeymoon (which, according to arrangement, was to be limited to one day).

The wedding-breakfast – two covers – at the magnificent, many-floored, music-enlivened, swarming Lyons' establishment in

15 Oxford Street had been – he was prepared to believe – relatively cheap, and there were no tips, and everything was very good and splendid; but really the bill amounted to a lot of money in the judgement of a man who for years had never spent more than sixpence on a meal outside his own home, and whom the mere

20 appearance of luxury frightened. Throughout the wedding-breakfast he had indeed been scared by the gilding, the carving, the seemingly careless profusion, the noise, and the vastness of

the throng which flung its money about in futile extravagance; he
had been unable to dismiss the disturbing notion that England
25 was decadent, and the structure of English society threatened by
a canker which had destroyed Gibbon's Rome. Ten shillings and
seven-pence for a single repast for two persons! It was fantastic.
He had resolved that this should be the last pleasure excursion
into the West End. Meanwhile, he was on his honeymoon, and
30 he must conduct himself and his purse with the chivalry which a
loved woman would naturally, if foolishly, expect.

It was after the wedding-breakfast that Violet had, in true
feminine capriciousness, suddenly suggested that they should go
to Madame Tussaud's wax-works before the visit to the gorgeous
35 cinema in Kingsway, which was the *pièce de résistance* of the
day's programme. She had never seen Madame Tussaud's (nor
had he), and she was sure it must be a very nice place; and they
had plenty of time for it. All her life she had longed to see
Madame Tussaud's, but somehow ... etc. Not that he needed too
40 much persuading. No! He liked, he adored the girlishness in that
vivacious but dignified and mature creature, so soberly dressed
(save for the exciting red flowers in her dark hat). In consenting
to gratify her whim he had the sensations of a young millionaire
clasping emerald necklaces round the divine necks of stage-
45 favourites. After all, it was only for one day. And she had spoken
truly in saying that they had plenty of time. The programme was
not to end till late. Previous to their departure from Riceyman
Steps on the wedding journey he had seen Violet call aside Elsie
(who was left in charge of the shop), and he doubted not that she
50 had been enjoining the girl to retire to bed before her employers'
return. A nice thoughtfulness on Violet's part.

Withal, as he extracted a pound note from his case, he suffered
agony – and she was watching him with her bright eyes. It was a
new pound note. The paper was white and substantial; not a
55 crease in it. The dim watermarks whispered genuineness. The
green and brown of the design were more beautiful than any
picture. The majestic representation of the Houses of Parliament
on the back gave assurance that the solidity of the whole realm
was behind that note. The thing was as lovely and touching as a
60 young virgin daughter. Could he abandon it for ever to the cold,
harsh world?

"Here! Give it me," said Violet sympathetically, and took it out
of his hand. What was she going to do with it?

"I've got change," she added, with a smile, her face crinkling
65 pleasantly.

Arnold Bennett

4.1

Make a list of what Henry and Violet do, where, and how much each
part of the day costs.

4.2

What are Henry's feelings in each place they visit? How much can you
tell about his past life?

4.3

Check any words or expressions you have difficulty with. Here are four which may give you problems:

turnstile – A revolving gate that admits/lets out one person at a time.

Lyons' – A chain of tea rooms all over Britain; although of good quality, there was nothing very 'magnificent' about them.

Gibbon – The well-known 18th century English author of *History of the Decline and Fall of the Roman Empire*.

Madame Tussaud's – London's famous museum of wax figures representing major historical/contemporary events and characters.

4.4

How many expressions can you find which mean 'spending'?

4.5

Words like 'futile' (line 23) and 'foolishly' (line 31) tell us something about Henry. Compare your impressions of him with what others in the class think. Then find words which tell us something about Violet. Who do you sympathize with more, Henry or Violet?

4.6

Who thinks 'What was she going to do with it?' (line 63)? What other indications are there of a personal point of view?

4.7

Do you find the passage realistic, or exaggerated? Have you yourself ever felt worried about how much you were spending, or felt you had to spend a lot to make a good impression? Compare your feelings with those described in the passage.

Discussion

There are lots of phrases in English which refer to money – sometimes realistically, sometimes symbolically. Discuss what you think these expressions mean. Are there similar expressions in your own language?

In for a penny, in for a pound.
Believe not much them that seem to despise riches.
Business is other people's money.
Every man has his price.
Money, like death, is still one of the great taboo subjects.
Put money in thy purse.
You pays your money and you takes your choice.
You can't take it with you.
Money talks.

5 📼

Finally we have an example of an extreme love of money. Volpone loves his money, hoards it, indeed even worships it in exaggerated images recalling the sun, the gods, and all kinds of power. As you read and listen, pick out expressions which confirm this idea of worship or reverence.

from VOLPONE

Volpone Good morning to the day; and next, my gold!
    Open the shrine, that I may see my saint.

[Mosca draws a curtain, and reveals piles of gold, plate, jewels, etc.]

    Hail, the world's soul, and mine! More glad than is
    The teeming earth to see the longed-for sun
5 Peep through the horns of the celestial Ram,
    Am I, to view thy splendour, darkening his;
    That, lying here amongst my other hoards,
    Show'st like a flame by night, or like the day
    Struck out of chaos, when all darkness fled
10 Unto the centre. O thou son of Sol
    (But brighter than thy father), let me kiss,
    With adoration, thee, and every relic
    Of sacred treasure in this blessed room.
    Well did wise poets by thy glorious name
15 Title that age which they would have the best –
    Thou being the best of things, and far transcending
    All style of joy in children, parents, friends,
    Or any other waking dream on earth.
    Thy looks when they to Venus did ascribe,
20 They should have given her twenty thousand Cupids:
    Such are thy beauties and our loves! Dear saint,
    Riches, the dumb god that giv'st all men tongues;
    That canst do nought and yet mak'st men do all things;
    The price of souls; even hell, with thee to boot,
25 Is made worth heaven. Thou art virtue, fame,
    Honour, and all things else. Who can get thee,
    He shall be noble, valiant, honest, wise –

Mosca And what he will, sir. Riches are in fortune
    A greater good than wisdom is in nature.

Ben Jonson

5.1 _____

What do the following words and expressions refer to?
mine (line 3), more glad (line 3), his (line 6), that (line 7), this (line 13), the best (line 15), thy looks (line 19), dear saint (line 21), he (line 28)

5.2 _____

Gold is contrasted very frequently with **a** light and **b** the sun. Find examples of either **a** or **b**.

5.3

Can you explain the following expressions in your own words?

far transcending all style of joy (lines 16 – 17)
any other waking dream (line 18)
the dumb god that giv'st all men tongues (line 22)
the price of souls (line 24)

5.4

What does this 'prayer' have in common with Lawrence's *Modern Prayer*?

5.5

How well does Beardsley's illustration at the beginning of this chapter catch the tone of the speech? What elements make the speech:
a dramatic; **b** visual?

5.6

Do Mosca's words confirm or contradict Volpone's, in your opinion?

Graffiti

Money speaks sense in a language all nations understand.
Aphra Behn

One must be poor to know the luxury of giving.
George Eliot

We may see the small value God has for riches by the people he gives them to.
Alexander Pope

Tasks

1 What are the attitudes to money in each of the texts you have read? Try to describe each in just one or two adjectives.
2 Write one or two paragraphs, highlighting points in common and differences in the texts you have read. Then, if you like, add your own comments and ideas on 'the best of things'.

Rehearse me in the parts
I must play

No man is an Island, entire of
itself; every man is a piece of the
Continent, a part of the main.

John Donne

Could you exist alone in the
world?

Why do you want, or need, other
people in your life?

Do you agree with the quotation
from John Donne?

How many people know the real
you?

1 📼

As you read the first text, try to
decide what has happened.

NOT WAVING BUT DROWNING

Nobody heard him, the dead man,
But still he lay moaning:
I was much further out than you thought
And not waving but drowning.

5 Poor chap, he always loved larking
And now he's dead
It must have been too cold for him his heart gave way,
They said.

Oh, no no no, it was too cold always
10 (Still the dead one lay moaning)
I was much too far out all my life
And not waving but drowning.

Stevie Smith

1.1 _____

Who is speaking in each verse?

1.2 _____

What does 'no no no' (line 9) refer to?

1.3 _____

What do 'much further out than you thought' (line 3) and 'much too far out' (line 11) refer to?

1.4 _____

Who is 'him/he' (lines 1 – 2) as opposed to 'I/you' (line 3)?

1.5 _____

Was he really 'larking' (line 5)?

1.6 _____

Whose comment is line 10? Why is it in parentheses?

1.7 _____

Which of the following words best describes for you what the poem is about?

loneliness   misunderstanding   pretending   suffering   indifference

1.8 _____

Who do you sympathize with?

2 📟

People often give themselves airs and take themselves very seriously. Charles Dickens is particularly good at portraying this sort of character. Here is one of his immortal egoists, Mr Podsnap. As you read, see if you can pick out some other aspects of Mr Podsnap's character.

from OUR MUTUAL FRIEND

Mr Podsnap was well to do, and stood very high in Mr Podsnap's opinion. Beginning with a good inheritance, he had married a good inheritance, and had thriven exceedingly in the Marine Insurance way, and was quite satisfied. He never could
5 make out why everybody was not quite satisfied, and he felt conscious that he set a brilliant social example in being particularly well satisfied with most things, and, above all other things, with himself.

Thus happily acquainted with his own merit and importance,
10 Mr Podsnap settled that whatever he put behind him he put out of existence. There was a dignified conclusiveness – not to add a grand convenience – in this way of getting rid of disagreeables, which had done much towards establishing Mr Podsnap in his lofty place in Mr Podsnap's satisfaction. "I don't want to know
15 about it; I don't choose to discuss it; I don't admit it!" Mr Podsnap had even acquired a peculiar flourish of his right arm in often clearing the world of its most difficult problems, by sweeping them behind him (and consequently sheer away) with

those words and a flushed face. For they affronted him.

20   Mr Podsnap's world was not a very large world, morally; no, nor even geographically: seeing that although his business was sustained upon commerce with other countries, he considered other countries, with that important reservation, a mistake, and of their manners and customs would conclusively observe, "Not

25 English!" when PRESTO! with a flourish of the arm, and a flush of the face, they were swept away. Elsewise, the world got up at eight, shaved close at a quarter-past, breakfasted at nine, went to the City at ten, came home at half-past five, and dined at seven. Mr Podsnap's notions of the Arts in their integrity might have

30 been stated thus. Literature; large print, respectively descriptive of getting up at eight, shaving close at a quarter-past, breakfasting at nine, going to the City at ten, coming home at half-past five, and dining at seven. Painting and Sculpture; models and portraits representing Professors of getting up at

35 eight, shaving close at a quarter-past, breakfasting at nine, going to the City at ten, coming home at half-past five, and dining at seven. Music; a respectable performance (without variations) on stringed and wind instruments, sedately expressive of getting up at eight, shaving close at a quarter-past, breakfasting at nine,

40 going to the City at ten, coming home at half-past five, and dining at seven. Nothing else to be permitted to those same vagrants the Arts, on pain of excommunication. Nothing else To Be – anywhere!

  As a so eminently respectable man, Mr Podsnap was sensible of

45 its being required of him to take Providence under his protection. Consequently he always knew exactly what Providence meant. Inferior and less respectable men might fall short of that mark, but Mr Podsnap was always up to it. And it was very remarkable (and must have been very comfortable) that

50 what Providence meant, was invariably what Mr Podsnap meant.

  These may be said to have been the articles of a faith and school which the present chapter takes the liberty of calling, after its representative man, Podsnappery. They were confined within close bounds, as Mr Podsnap's own head was confined by

55 his shirt-collar; and they were enunciated with a sounding pomp that smacked of the creaking of Mr Podsnap's own boots.

Charles Dickens

2.1 ⎯⎯⎯⎯⎯⎯⎯⎯⎯⎯⎯⎯⎯⎯⎯⎯⎯⎯⎯⎯⎯⎯⎯⎯⎯⎯

The first paragraph tells us about Mr Podsnap's attitude to himself. Which words would you choose as key-words to describe him?

2.2 ⎯⎯⎯⎯⎯⎯⎯⎯⎯⎯⎯⎯⎯⎯⎯⎯⎯⎯⎯⎯⎯⎯⎯⎯⎯⎯

'Mr Podsnap's attitude to himself' could be used as a heading for paragraph 1. Find similar headings for the next four paragraphs. Then choose one or two key-words from each paragraph.

2.3

Sum up Mr Podsnap's ideas on:
– other countries
– the Arts
– Providence

2.4

What does 'that important reservation' in line 23 refer back to?

2.5

Repetition plays an important part in this passage. Underline all the expressions that are repeated, or in some way echo one another.

2.6

At the beginning of this extract we read 'Mr Podsnap was well to do, and stood very high in Mr Podsnap's opinion.' In normal English we would have expected:

'... and stood very high in his own opinion.'
or '... and had a very good opinion of himself.'

By repeating 'Mr Podsnap' in this way Dickens surprises us; he defeats our expectations. This is an example of the author commenting ironically on one of his characters, and it encourages us to look at Mr Podsnap in an ironical way. Another example of this is the use of 'a good inheritance' (line 3) instead of 'a good wife'. Pick out more phrases, nouns, verbs, adjectives or adverbs which reveal the author's ironic tone in the passage.

2.7

Now pick out some of the many heavy, long-winded words which account for the undercurrent of humour.

2.8

Write a short paragraph listing the 'articles of Podsnappery' in your own words.

3 📼

Sometimes a person can have a double identity: the most famous case is Stevenson's *Dr Jekyll and Mr Hyde*. Here the metamorphosis from Hyde to Jekyll, described by Hastie Lanyon in a letter to a friend, Mr Utterson, is taking place before our very eyes. As you read and listen, pick out where the narration changes from description to reflection.

from THE STRANGE CASE OF DR JEKYLL AND MR HYDE

He put the glass to his lips and drank at one gulp. A cry followed; he reeled, staggered, clutched at the table and held on, staring with injected eyes, gasping with open mouth; and as I looked there came, I thought, a change – he seemed to swell –
5 his face became suddenly black and the features seemed to melt and alter – and the next moment, I had sprung to my feet and leaped back against the wall, my arm raised to shield me from that prodigy, my mind submerged in terror.
   "O God!" I screamed, and "O God!" again and again; for there
10 before my eyes – pale and shaken, and half fainting, and groping before him with his hands, like a man restored from death – there stood Henry Jekyll!
   What he told me in the next hour, I cannot bring my mind to set on paper. I saw what I saw, I heard what I heard, and my soul
15 sickened at it; and yet now when that sight has faded from my eyes, I ask myself if I believe it, and I cannot answer. My life is shaken to its roots; sleep has left me; the deadliest terror sits by me at all hours of the day and night; I feel that my days are numbered, and that I must die; and yet I shall die incredulous. As

> 20 for the moral turpitude that man unveiled to me, even with tears
> of penitence, I cannot, even in memory, dwell on it without a start
> of horror. I will say but one thing, Utterson, and that (if you can
> bring your mind to credit it) will be more than enough. The
> creature who crept into my house that night was, on Jekyll's own
> 25 confession, known by the name of Hyde and hunted for in every
> corner of the land as the murderer of Carew.
>
> *Robert Louis Stevenson*

3.1

'I saw what I saw' refers to lines 1 to 12. Report the scene in its visual elements only.

3.2

What, in turn, does, 'I heard what I heard' refer to? Find as many references as you can in the passage to the 'heard' or 'spoken' elements of the scene.

3.3

The onlooker/narrator, Hastie Lanyon, adds distance and objectivity to the scene described, recounting the metamorphosis to Mr Utterson, the lawyer.   Yet his emotional involvement emerges through a number of actions and expressions. Pick out as many as you can.

3.4

Do you find the description of the 'change' convincing, credible, exaggerated, grotesque, ridiculous, realistic, powerful, or anything different? Give reasons for your answers.

3.5

Can people be totally good or totally bad, do you think? List your arguments in two columns, and discuss them in groups.

3.6

Do you think everyone has a kind of split personality – not as exaggerated perhaps as Jekyll and Hyde, but representing aspects of their character? Discuss what aspects Jekyll or Hyde might underline.

4

CHARLES

In this short story, the author draws a picture of the young Charles as reflected through the eyes of his schoolmate Laurie, another small boy just beginning kindergarten. Charles, it seems, is naughty, rude and free-spirited, almost always noisy and a trouble to the teacher. By comparison, Laurie appears well-behaved. His mother looks forward to meeting Charles's mother. What a terrible strain it must be to be the parent of such a wild child...

The day my son Laurie started kindergarten he renounced corduroy overalls with bibs and began wearing blue jeans with a belt; I watched him go off the first morning with the older girl next door, seeing clearly that an era of my life was ended, my
5 sweet-voiced nursery-school tot replaced by a long-trousered, swaggering character who forgot to stop at the corner and wave good-bye to me.

He came home the same way, the front door slamming open, his cap on the floor, and the voice suddenly become raucous
10 shouting, "Isn't anybody here?"

At lunch he spoke insolently to his father, spilled his baby sister's milk, and remarked that his teacher said we were not to take the name of the Lord in vain.

"How *was* school today?" I asked, elaborately casual.
15 "All right," he said.

"Did you learn anything?" his father asked.

Laurie regarded his father coldly. "I didn't learn nothing," he said.

"Anything," I said. "Didn't learn anything."
20 "The teacher spanked a boy, though," Laurie said, addressing his bread and butter. "For being fresh," he added with his mouth full.

"What did he do?" I asked. "Who was it?"

Laurie thought. "It was Charles," he said. "He was fresh. The
25 teacher spanked him and made him stand in a corner. He was awfully fresh."

"What did he do?" I asked again, but Laurie slid off his chair, took a cookie, and left, while his father was still saying, "See here, young man."
30 The next day Laurie remarked at lunch, as soon as he sat down, "Well, Charles was bad again today." He grinned enormously and said, "Today Charles hit the teacher."

"Good heavens," I said, mindful of the Lord's name, "I suppose he got spanked again?"
35 "He sure did," Laurie said. "Look up," he said to his father.

"What?" his father said, looking up.

"Look down," Laurie said. "Look at my thumb. Gee, you're dumb." He began to laugh insanely.

"Why did Charles hit the teacher?" I asked quickly.
40 "Because she tried to make him color with red crayons," Laurie said.

"Charles wanted to color with green crayons, so he hit the teacher and she spanked him and said nobody play with Charles but everybody did."
45 The third day – it was Wednesday of the first week – Charles bounced a seesaw onto the head of a little girl and made her bleed, and the teacher made him stay inside all during recess. Thursday Charles had to stand in a corner during storytime because he kept pounding his feet on the floor. Friday Charles
50 was deprived of blackboard privileges because he threw chalk.

On Saturday I remarked to my husband, "Do you think kindergarten is too unsettling for Laurie? All this toughness and bad grammar, and this Charles boy sounds like such a bad influence."

55 "It'll be all right," my husband said reassuringly. "Bound to be people like Charles in the world. Might as well meet them now as later."

On Monday Laurie came home late, full of news. "Charles," he shouted as he came up the hill; I was waiting anxiously on the

60 front step. "Charles," Laurie yelled all the way up the hill, "Charles was bad again."

"Come right in," I said, as soon as he came close enough. "Lunch is waiting."

"You know what Charles did?" he demanded, following me

65 through the door, "Charles yelled so in school they sent a boy in from first grade to tell the teacher she had to make Charles keep quiet, and so Charles had to stay after school. And so all the children stayed to watch him."

"What did he do?" I asked.

70 "He just sat there," Laurie said, climbing into his chair at the table. "Hi, Pop, y'old dust mop."

"Charles had to stay after school today," I told my husband. "Everyone stayed with him."

"What does this Charles look like?" my husband asked Laurie.

75 "What's his other name?"

"He's bigger than me," Laurie said. "And he doesn't have any rubbers and he doesn't ever wear a jacket."

Monday night was the first Parent-Teachers meeting, and only the fact that the baby had a cold kept me from going; I wanted

80 passionately to meet Charles's mother. On Tuesday Laurie remarked suddenly, "Our teacher had a friend come see her in school today."

"Charles's mother?" my husband and I asked simultaneously.

"Naah," Laurie said scornfully. "It was a man who came and

85 made us do exercises; we had to touch our toes. Look." He climbed down from his chair and squatted down and touched his toes. "Like this," he said, picking up his fork, "Charles didn't even *do* exercises."

"That's fine," I said heartily. "Didn't Charles want to do

90 exercises?"

"Naaah," Laurie said. "Charles was so fresh to the teacher's friend he wasn't *let* do exercises."

"Fresh again?" I said.

"He kicked the teacher's friend," Laurie said. "The teacher's

95 friend told Charles to touch his toes like I just did, and Charles kicked him."

"What are they going to do about Charles, do you suppose?" Laurie's father asked him.

Laurie shrugged elaborately. "Throw him out of school, I

100 guess," he said.

Wednesday and Thursday were routine; Charles yelled during story hour and hit a boy in the stomach and made him cry. On Friday Charles stayed after school again, and so did all the other children.

105   With the third week of kindergarten Charles was an institution in our family; the baby was being a Charles when she cried all afternoon; Laurie did a Charles when he filled his wagon full of mud and pulled it through the kitchen; even my husband, when he caught his elbow in the telephone cord and pulled telephone,
110 ash tray, and a bowl of flowers off the table, said, after the first minute, "Looks like Charles."

During the third and fourth weeks it looked like a reformation in Charles; Laurie reported grimly at lunch on Thursday of the third week, "Charles was so good today the teacher gave him an
115 apple."

"What?" I said, and my husband added warily, "You mean Charles?"

"Charles," Laurie said. "He gave the crayons around and he picked up the books afterward and the teacher said he was her
120 helper."

"What happened?" I asked incredulously.

"He was her helper, that's all," Laurie said, and shrugged.

"Can this be true, about Charles?" I asked my husband that night. "Can something like this happen?"
125   "Wait and see," my husband said cynically. "When you've got a Charles to deal with, this may mean he's only plotting."

He seemed to be wrong. For over a week Charles was the teacher's helper; each day he handed things out and he picked things up; no one had to stay after school.
130   "The P.T.A. meeting's next week again," I told my husband one evening. "I'm going to find Charles's mother there."

"Ask her what happened to Charles," my husband said. "I'd like to know."

"I'd like to know myself," I said.
135   On Friday of that week things were back to normal. "You know what Charles did today?" Laurie demanded at the lunch table, in a voice slightly awed. "He told a little girl to say a word and she said it and the teacher washed her mouth out with soap and Charles laughed."
140   "What word?" his father asked unwisely, and Laurie said, "I'll have to whisper it to you, it's so bad." He got down off his chair and went around to his father. His father bent his head down and Laurie whispered joyfully. His father's eyes widened.

"Did Charles tell the little girl to say *that*?" he asked
145 respectfully.

"She said it *twice*," Laurie said. "Charles told her to say it *twice*."

"What happened to Charles?" my husband asked.

"Nothing," Laurie said. "He was passing out the crayons."

Monday morning Charles abandoned the little girl and said the
150 evil word himself three or four times, getting his mouth washed out with soap each time. He also threw chalk.

My husband came to the door with me that evening as I set out for the P.T.A. meeting. "Invite her over for a cup of tea after the meeting," he said. "I want to get a look at her."
155   "If only she's there," I said prayerfully.

"She'll be there," my husband said. " I don't see how they could hold a P.T.A. meeting without Charles's mother."

At the meeting I sat restlessly, scanning each comfortable matronly face, trying to determine which one hid the secret of
160 Charles. None of them looked to me haggard enough. No one stood up in the meeting and apologized for the way her son had been acting. No one mentioned Charles.

After the meeting I identified and sought out Laurie's kindergarten teacher. She had a plate with a cup of tea and a
165 piece of chocolate cake; I had a plate with a cup of tea and a piece of marshmallow cake. We maneuvered up to one another cautiously, and smiled.

"I've been so anxious to meet you," I said. "I'm Laurie's mother."
170 "We're all so interested in Laurie," she said.

"Well, he certainly likes kindergarten," I said. "He talks about it all the time."

"We had a little trouble adjusting, the first week or so," she said primly, "but now he's a fine little helper. With occasional lapses,
175 of course."

"Laurie usually adjusts very quickly," I said. "I suppose this time it's Charles's influence."

"Charles?"

"Yes," I said laughing, " you must have your hands full in that
180 kindergarten, with Charles."

"Charles?" she said. "We don't have any Charles in the kindergarten."

Shirley Jackson

4.1

Laurie's behaviour mirrors Charles's all the way through. List examples of mischief and punishment which the teacher refers to by saying 'We had a little trouble adjusting, the first week or so'. (line 173)

4.2

Now find instances of what the teacher calls 'occasional lapses'.
(line 174)

4.3

Select:
a a few 'tough', rude or incorrect expressions used by Laurie;
b some examples of 'free-spirited' behaviour, which his parents blame on Charles's bad influence.

4.4

Why are 'Parent-Teachers' (line 78) spelt with a capital letter? What does P.T.A. stand for?

4.5
_____

What clues can you find to the cultural background of the story? Here are a few, to start you going. Pick them out in the text, and find some more.

kindergarten   color
fresh   first grade
cookie   rubbers
gee

4.6
_____

Expand the ideas contained in:

grimly (line 113)   warily (line 116)
haggard (line 160)   elaborately (lines 14 and 99)
primly (line 174)   respectfully (line 145)

4.7
_____

Pick out at lcast four examples of colloquialisms.

4.8
_____

Why do you think the teacher says 'We're all so interested in Laurie' ? (line 170)

4.9
_____

Describe your reaction to the last line of the story.

4.10
_____

What aspects of children's psychology does the story illustrate? Here are some possibilities for you to consider, exclude, accept, or add to. Give reasons for your answers.

need to be taken into consideration   difficulty in adjusting
refusal to grow up   longing to be cared for
refusal to comply with rules   creativity
fear of novelty and changes   inventiveness
lack of self-confidence   confusing facts and imagination
diffidence   peculiar sense of humour

Discussion

How do people's opinions affect your behaviour? Why do we tell lies, invent excuses, hide behind masks, pretend we are different from what we are, create and promote our image? Do we know ourselves for what we really are, with our good and bad qualities, our strong or vulnerable points?

5 📼

PRAYER BEFORE BIRTH

I am not yet born; O hear me.
Let not the bloodsucking bat or the rat or the stoat or the
    club-footed ghoul come near me.

I am not yet born, console me.
5 I fear that the human race may with tall walls wall me,
    with strong drugs dope me, with wise lies lure me,
      on black racks rack me, in blood-baths roll me.

I am not yet born; provide me
With water to dandle me, grass to grow for me, trees to talk
10   to me, sky to sing to me, birds and a white light
      in the back of my mind to guide me.

I am not yet born, forgive me
For the sins that in me the world shall commit, my words
    when they speak me, my thoughts when they think me,
15   my treason engendered by traitors beyond me,
        my life when they murder by means of my
          hands, my death when they live me.

I am not yet born; rehearse me
In the parts I must play and the cues I must take when
20   old men lecture me, bureaucrats hector me, mountains
      frown at me, lovers laugh at me, the white
        waves call me to folly and the desert calls
          me to doom and the beggar refuses
            my gift and my children curse me.

25 I am not yet born; O hear me,
Let not the man who is beast or who thinks he is God
    come near me.

I am not yet born; O fill me
With strength against those who would freeze my
30   humanity, would dragoon me into a lethal automaton,
      would make me a cog in a machine, a thing with
        one face, a thing, and against all those
          who would dissipate my entirety, would
            blow me like thistledown hither and
35   thither or hither and thither
                like water held in the
                  hands would spill me.

Let them not make me a stone and let them not spill me.
Otherwise kill me.

Louis MacNeice

Louis MacNeice takes his psychological exploration of identity even further back. As you read and listen, decide who is speaking. Consider why the speaker might be frightened by the prospect of taking on an identity.

5.1

On first reading, which lines strike you most?

5.2 _____

Pick out some lines or phrases which are particularly easy to understand, and discuss whether they are positive or negative.

5.3 _____

Now look at some of the more difficult lines. Make a list of them, and try to explain each with the help of your dictionary. Does this help you to understand the speaker's fears better? Which of the lines or phrases seem to you to be particularly effective, obscure, memorable?

5.4 _____

Find images connected with the following ideas, and match each one with the relevant verse.

a longing for freedom
b fear of being made insensitive or being wasted
c fear of life in general, of experience
d prayer for indulgence
e fear of animals
f longing for nature and knowledge

5.5 _____

How do the lay-out of the poem and the rhyme pattern contribute to its effectiveness?

5.6 _____

Do you think the last line implies an attitude towards abortion? Could the poem be intended as a justification for such an act?

Graffiti

There will be time, there will be time
To prepare a face to meet the faces that you meet.
T.S.Eliot

Most people are other people. Their thoughts are someone else's opinions, their lives a mimicry, their passions a quotation.
Oscar Wilde

Tasks

1 Write a few paragraphs about yourself, i.e. the way you perceive yourself, but preferably in the third person singular, to make it more objective and memorable, and possibly in the past tense, for extra detachment.

2 Write a short composition about somebody you would like to be – a famous star, an historical character, a friend you admire, etc. Use some of the ideas that came up in the discussions with your group to support your argument.

Time on the clock and time in the mind

How long is 'forever'?
Can you say what 'infinity' is?
Words cannot always express
such concepts fully, but some
people like to think that the colour
blue, for example, represents
infinity. Why do you think they
choose blue? Do you agree? What
other colours can represent ideas,
for you?

---

1 📼

As you read this poem by Ernest
Dowson, what are your immediate
impressions as to what he is
talking about?

VITAE SUMMA BREVIS SPEM
NOS VETAT INCOHARE LONGAM

> They are not long, the weeping and the laughter,
>   Love and desire and hate:
> I think they have no portion in us after
>   We pass the gate.
>
> 5 They are not long, the days of wine and roses:
>   Out of a misty dream
> Our path emerges for a while, then closes
>   Within a dream.
>
> *Ernest Dowson*

1.1 —

By saying 'they are not long', do you think the poet is being positive or
negative, optimistic or pessimistic?

1.2 _____

Why do you think Dowson says 'the weeping and the laughter' (line 1), but uses no definite article with 'love', 'desire' and 'hate' in line 2?

1.3 _____

What do you think 'we pass the gate' (4) and 'our path' (7) are metaphors for?

1.4 _____

Is line 5 more or less positive than line 1, in your opinion?

1.5 _____

What do the last three lines refer to?

1.6 _____

The poem has a Latin title, taken from the poet Horace, meaning 'the brevity of life prevents us from planning ahead' – Vitae summa brevis spem nos vetat incohare longam. Do you think it is a good title? Why? Why not?

1.7 _____

Tick the adjectives which you think best describe the overall tone of the poem and justify your choice(s).

soppy	detached
relieved	dreamy
resigned	self-pitying
gloomy	sad
regretful	indulgent

2 📼
_____

The next two texts continue the idea of 'passing time'. As you read and listen to them, what can you say of the writers' attitudes to their lover?

WHEN YOU GO

When you go,
if you go,
and I should want to die,
there's nothing I'd be saved by
5   more than the time
you fell asleep in my arms
in a trust so gentle
I let the darkening room
drink up the evening, till
10   rest, or the new rain
lightly roused you awake.
I asked if you heard the rain in your dream
and half dreaming still you only said, I love you.

Edwin Morgan

ERAT HORA

> "Thank you, whatever comes." And then she turned
> And, as the ray of sun on hanging flowers
> Fades when the wind hath lifted them aside,
> Went swiftly from me. Nay, whatever comes
> 5 One hour was sunlit and the most high gods
> May not make boast of any better thing
> Than to have watched that hour as it passed.
>
> *Ezra Pound*

2.1

Is the poet alone in the first poem? Who is he speaking to? Are they still lovers?

2.2

Describe in your own words the idea expressed in the poem.

2.3

Erat Hora means 'It was time' or 'There was a time'. Would you prefer an English title – if so, which one, and why?

2.4

Who do you think speaks the first four words of the second poem? What does 'Thank you' refer to? What was good before 'she turned And ... Went'?

2.5

How is the simile of lines 2 and 3 connected with the woman's leaving?

2.6

How does the poet feel in relation to 'the most high gods' (line 5)?

2.7

When You Go and *Erat Hora* both find something positive in a negative idea. Something makes the separation acceptable. Try to say what it is in each case, and why the memory of these moments will remain.

3 🎦

from MACBETH

As you read the famous summing-up of life and time which Macbeth gives near the end of his life, make a note of references to past, present and future.

Seyton
The Queen, my Lord, is dead.

Macbeth
She should have died hereafter.
There would have been a time for such a word.
To-morrow, and to-morrow, and to-morrow,
5 Creeps in this petty pace from day to day
To the last syllable of recorded time,
And all our yesterdays have lighted fools
The way to dusty death. Out, out, brief candle!
Life's but a walking shadow, a poor player,
10 That struts and frets his hour upon the stage,
And then is heard no more; it is a tale
Told by an idiot, full of sound and fury,
Signifying nothing.

William Shakespeare

3.1 ⎯⎯⎯⎯⎯⎯⎯⎯⎯⎯⎯⎯⎯⎯⎯⎯⎯⎯⎯

Who or what do you normally expect to 'creep'? What do you usually associate the words 'syllable' and 'recorded' with? Try to find more examples where words are used in a context that contrasts with what we might usually expect.

3.2 ⎯⎯⎯⎯⎯⎯⎯⎯⎯⎯⎯⎯⎯⎯⎯⎯⎯⎯⎯

Does the image of the candle refer to life in general or to Lady Macbeth, whose death has only just been announced? What word in the previous line prepares for it?

3.3 ⎯⎯⎯⎯⎯⎯⎯⎯⎯⎯⎯⎯⎯⎯⎯⎯⎯⎯⎯

Is the 'stage' metaphor a good one to mean life? How and why?

3.4 ⎯⎯⎯⎯⎯⎯⎯⎯⎯⎯⎯⎯⎯⎯⎯⎯⎯⎯⎯

Choose one or two adjectives from among the following, supporting your choice, to define the tone of the speech:

negative	disillusioned
desperate	pessimistic
tragic	sad
bitter	impassioned
low-spirited	disheartened

4

The next text plays with time in a fascinating way – as the writer describes the character's thoughts, time expands and contracts. As you read, make note of the changes in time, and the way the writer tells us about them.

from ORLANDO

Here he came then, day after day, week after week, month after month, year after year. He saw the beech trees turn golden and the young ferns unfurl; he saw the moon sickle and then circular; he saw – but probably the reader can imagine the passage which
5 should follow and how every tree and plant in the neighbourhood is described first green, then golden; how moons rise and suns set; how spring follows winter and autumn summer; how night succeeds day and day night; how there is first a storm and then fine weather; how things remain much as they are for two or
10 three hundred years or so, except for a little dust and a few cobwebs which one old woman can sweep up in half an hour; a conclusion which, one cannot help feeling, might have been reached more quickly by the simple statement that "Time passed" (here the exact amount could be indicated in brackets)
15 and nothing whatever happened.
    But Time, unfortunately, though it makes animals and vegetables bloom and fade with amazing punctuality, has no such simple effect upon the mind of man. The mind of man, moreover, works with equal strangeness upon the body of time. An hour,
20 once it lodges in the queer element of the human spirit, may be stretched to fifty or a hundred times its clock length; on the other hand, an hour may be accurately represented on the timepiece of the mind by one second. This extraordinary discrepancy between time on the clock and time in the mind is

25 less known than it should be and deserves fuller investigation.
But the biographer, whose interests are, as we have said, highly
restricted, must confine himself to one simple statement: when a
man has reached the age of thirty, as Orlando now had, time
when he is thinking becomes inordinately long; time when he is
30 doing becomes inordinately short. Thus Orlando gave his orders
and did the business of his vast estates in a flash; but directly he
was alone on the mound under the oak tree, the seconds began
to round and fill until it seemed as if they would never fall. They
filled themselves, moreover, with the strangest variety of objects.
35 For not only did he find himself confronted by problems which
have puzzled the wisest of men, such as What is love? What
friendship? What truth? but directly he came to think about
them, his whole past, which seemed to him of extreme length
and variety, rushed into the falling second, swelled it a dozen
40 times its natural size, coloured it a thousand tints, and filled it
with all the odds and ends in the universe.

In such thinking (or by whatever name it should be called) he
spent months and years of his life. It would be no exaggeration to
say that he would go out after breakfast a man of thirty and come
45 home to dinner a man of fifty-five at least. Some weeks added a
century to his age, others no more than three seconds at most.

Virginia Woolf

4.1

Match the following words in the text with their equivalents:

unfurl (line 3)	thin as a curved blade
sickle (line 3)	swell
lodges (line 20)	open up
queer (line 20)	the moment/as soon as
discrepancy (line 24)	small unimportant objects
directly (lines 31 and 37)	strange
round and fill (line 33)	gap/difference
odds and ends (line 41)	is contained

4.2

Is it possible to say how much time passes in the course of the passage?
Why/why not?

4.3

What contrasts between people/animals and vegetables can you find?
What do they tell us about time?

4.4

Can you tell anything about Orlando from this passage? What is it
actually about?

4.5 _____

Can you describe the difference between 'time on the clock' and 'time in the mind' in your own words? Have you ever felt this kind of 'fluctuation' of time? Discuss how real the idea is, and compare your conclusions with the rest of the group.

Discussion

The Well-Wrought Urn

"What would you do if I suddenly died?"
"Write a poem to you."
"Would you mourn for me?"
"Certainly," I sighed.
"For a long time?"
"That depends."
"On what?"
"The poem's excellence," I replied.

Irvin Layton

Do you agree that poetry/art can defeat time and give immortality to the poet/artist?

5 🔲

This famous ode by John Keats is about the power of art to preserve, outside time, intense human experiences, so that they pass on their message of beauty and happiness to people from one generation to another. As you read and listen, try to select images related to music, love and time.

ODE ON A GRECIAN URN

Thou still unravish'd bride of quietness,
Thou foster-child of Silence and slow Time,
Sylvan historian, who canst thus express
A flowery tale more sweetly than our rhyme:
5 What leaf-fringed legend haunts about thy shape
Of deities or mortals, or of both,
In Tempe or the dales of Arcady?
What men or gods are these? What maidens loth?
What mad pursuit? What struggle to escape?
10 What pipes and timbrels? What wild ecstasy?

Heard melodies are sweet, but those unheard
Are sweeter: therefore, ye soft pipes, play on;
Not to the sensual ear, but, more endear'd,
Pipe to the spirit ditties of no tone:
15 Fair youth, beneath the trees, thou canst not leave
Thy song, nor ever can those trees be bare;
Bold Lover, never, never canst thou kiss,
Though winning near the goal – yet, do not grieve;
She cannot fade, though thou hast not thy bliss,
20 For ever wilt thou love, and she be fair!

Ah, happy, happy boughs! that cannot shed
Your leaves, nor ever bid the Spring adieu;
And, happy melodist, unwearied,
Forever piping songs for ever new;
25 More happy love! more happy, happy love!

For ever warm and still to be enjoy'd,
For ever panting and for ever young;
All breathing human passion far above,
That leaves a heart high sorrowful and cloy'd,
30   A burning forehead, and a parching tongue.

Who are these coming to the sacrifice?
To what green altar, O mysterious priest,
Lead'st thou that heifer lowing at the skies,
And all her silken flanks with garlands drest?
35   What little town by river or sea-shore,
Or mountain-built with peaceful citadel,
Is emptied of his folk, this pious morn?
And, little town, thy streets for evermore
Will silent be; and not a soul to tell
40   Why thou art desolate, can e'er return.

O Attic shape! Fair attitude! with brede
Or marble men and maidens overwrought,
With forest branches and the trodden weed;
Thou, silent form, dost tease us out of thought
45   As doth eternity: Cold Pastoral!
When old age shall this generation waste,
Thou shalt remain, in midst of other woe
Than ours, a friend to man, to whom thou say'st,
"Beauty is truth, truth beauty – that is all
50   Ye know on earth, and all ye need to know."

John Keats

5.1

The urn tells a tale, like a historian, through the scene which is
represented on it. Why does the speaker call it 'sylvan historian'
(line 3)? What is the connection with 'flowery tale' (line 4) and
'leaf-fringed legend' (line 5)?

5.2

In lines 5 to 10 what does the speaker tell us about the scene on the
vase, as he asks his questions?

5.3

What two types of music does the speaker contrast in lines 11 to 14?

5.4

In lines 15 to 20 the speaker imagines the situation of the figures on the
urn; they cannot do certain things but have certain advantages.
Explain:

a what these advantages and disadvantages are
b what elements stress the idea of timelessness
c what the difference is between the lovers on the urn and lovers in
   real life

5.5

In the fourth verse we may suppose that the speaker has turned the urn round and is looking at the other side of the scene. What does he see here?

5.6

Which lines correspond to a scene which is not on the urn, but only imagined?

5.7

Try to establish:
a where you can perceive a new feeling in the poem
b which other quality of timelessness presents itself in the poem
c the meaning of lines 44 – 45

5.8

What do 'our rhyme' (line 4), 'tease us' (line 44), 'this generation' (line 46) indicate about the speaker? How far do you think this voice coincides with that of Keats?

5.9

As the speaker describes his feelings about the urn, do you find yourself sympathetic to what he is saying? Or do you disagree and find that you feel quite differently? Try to describe and explain your reactions.

Graffiti

Age cannot wither her, nor custom stale
Her infinite variety. Other women cloy
The appetites they feed, but she makes hungry
Where most she satisfies.
William Shakespeare

Nothing is eternal, alas, except eternity.
Paul Valery

Tasks

1 Imagine you wake up after fifty years' sleep. What would you find changed around you? Write a composition of 150 words describing what you see.
2 If you could stop time, which moments would you want to save and expand? Write short descriptive paragraphs about such moments on pieces of paper, and exchange them, anonymously, with others in the class.

Shining for me alone

In Chapter 7 we saw something of the difficulty of being alone – now, we are going to look at the difference between solitude and loneliness.

What do you think the difference is?

Can either of them have positive connotations?

Do you ever prefer to be alone? Why?

Can you feel alone when you are with another person? Discuss with the group how this can happen, and whether you can do anything to avoid it.

1

Consider this poem by Roger McGough. What do you think the title means? In what way does the typographical layout contribute to the meaning of the poem?

40 – LOVE

```
        40 –          love
        middle        aged
        couple        playing
        ten           nis
     5  when          the
        game          ends
        and           they
        go            home
        the           net
    10  will          still
        be            be
        tween         them
```

Roger McGough

1.1

What is the poem about – love, distance, separation, routine, loneliness, marriage, middle age, or anything else?

1.2

Does it remind you of any other text(s) in this book?

1.3

Does the poem strike you as being sad, witty, clever, amusing, disconcerting or not really poetry?

2 📼

William Wordsworth found his
loneliness interrupted and relieved
by a sight that remained ever
afterwards imprinted on his
'inward eye'. As you read, find how
many positive or happy words
there are.

DAFFODILS

I wandered lonely as a cloud
　　That floats on high o'er vales and hills.
When all at once I saw a crowd,
　　A host, of golden daffodils;
5 Beside the lake, beneath the trees,
Fluttering and dancing in the breeze.

Continuous as the stars that shine
　　And twinkle on the Milky Way,
They stretched in never-ending line
10　　Along the margin of a bay:
Ten thousand saw I at a glance,
Tossing their heads in sprightly dance.

The waves beside them danced, but they
　　Out-did the sparkling waves in glee:
15 A poet could not but be gay,
　　In such a jocund company:
I gazed – and gazed – but little thought
What wealth the show to me had brought.

For oft, when on my couch I lie
20　　In vacant or in pensive mood,
They flash upon that inward eye
　　Which is the bliss of solitude;
And then my heart with pleasure fills,
And dances with the daffodils.

William Wordsworth

2.1

List the verbs that indicate movement of the flowers and the waves.
What images do they create? What image do you have of the poet? How
do the verbs that relate to him contribute to that image?

2.2

What do you think he means by 'wealth' in 'What wealth the show to me
had brought' ? How does it affect his feelings when he recalls the scene?

2.3

What do you think the poet means by 'the bliss of solitude' (line 22)?
What is the 'inward eye' (line 21)? Discuss it with the group.

2.4

What feelings or themes can you find in the poem?

2.5

The poet speaks of himself a lot; indeed the whole poem is about a
personal experience. How do you react to this personal tone? Do you
feel interested, indifferent, excluded, irritated? Have you ever had a
similar experience yourself?

3 📼

Now consider the theme of
loneliness in this other poem by
Wordsworth.

SHE DWELT AMONG TH'UNTRODDEN WAYS

> She dwelt among th'untrodden ways
>   Beside the springs of Dove,
> A Maid whom there were none to praise
>   And very few to love.
>
> 5   A Violet by a mossy stone
>   Half-hidden from the Eye!
> – Fair, as a star when only one
>   Is shining in the sky!
>
> She liv'd unknown, and few could know
> 10   When Lucy ceas'd to be;
> But she is in her Grave, and Oh!
>   The difference to me.
>
> *William Wordsworth*

3.1

What effect does the use of 'she' instead of her name have on you?

3.2

Pick out the linguistically negative elements of the text, e.g. untrodden
(line 1), none (line 3), very few (line 4). Find some more. What would
their 'positive' counterparts be? Do they mean that Lucy was, for
example, poor, deprived of something, unfulfilled or unhappy?

3.3

What is Lucy compared to?

3.4

Discuss whether *Lucy* as a title would have been better. Are titles
important in poems?

3.5

Tell Lucy's story in a few words. What is your idea of this girl/woman?

3.6

What is the relationship between the poet and Lucy, and what was their
relationship in the past in your opinion?

3.7

Was loneliness a positive or negative thing to Lucy?

3.8

Consider these lines from *Ode to Solitude* by Alexander Pope:

Thus let me live unseen, unknown,
Thus unlamented let me die,
Steal from the world, and not a stone
Tell where I lie.

Discuss what Lucy and this speaker had in common, and in what way they differ. Then compare and contrast the two poems with *Daffodils* for a final consideration of loneliness/solitude.

4 📼

For some people the worst aspect of solitude is absence or lack of company. In the next story, the woman who is speaking is landlady to three young men, but still feels the need for company. Read the second half of the story first – from line 69. As you read and listen to the first paragraph of this part of the story, try to imagine what kind of company the 'he/him' she mentions represents. Then, as you read on, what impression do you get of the woman?

...You see that big nail to the right of the front door? I can scarcely look at it even now and yet I could not bear to take it out. I should like to think it was there always, even after my time. I sometimes hear the next people saying, "There must have been
5 a cage hanging from there." And it comforts me; I feel he is not quite forgotten.

...You cannot imagine how wonderfully he sang. It was not like the singing of other canaries. And that isn't just my fancy. Often, from the window, I used to see people stop at the gate to listen,
10 or they would lean over the fence by the mock-orange for quite a long time – carried away. I suppose it sounds absurd to you – it wouldn't if you had heard him – but it really seemed to me that he sang whole songs with a beginning and an end to them.

For instance, when I'd finished the house in the afternoon, and
15 changed my blouse and brought my sewing on to the veranda here, he used to hop, hop, hop from one perch to another, tap against the bars as if to attract my attention, sip a little water just as a professional singer might, and then break into a song so exquisite that I had to put my needle down to listen to him. I
20 can't describe it; I wish I could. But it was always the same, every afternoon, and I felt that I understood every note of it.

... I loved him. How I loved him! Perhaps it does not matter so very much what it is one loves in this world. But love something one must. Of course there was always my little house and the
25 garden, but for some reason they were never enough. Flowers respond wonderfully, but they don't sympathize. Then I loved the evening star. Does that sound foolish? I used to go into the backyard, after sunset, and wait for it until it shone above the dark gum tree. I used to whisper, "There you are, my darling."
30 And just in that first moment it seemed to be shining for me alone. It seemed to understand this ... something which is like longing, and yet it is not longing. Or regret – it is more like regret. And yet regret for what? I have much to be thankful for.

... But after he came into my life I forgot the evening star; I did
35 not need it anymore. But it was strange. When the Chinaman who came to the door with birds to sell held him up in his tiny cage, and instead of fluttering, fluttering, like the poor little goldfinches, he gave a faint, small chirp, I found myself saying, just as I had said to the star over the gum tree, "There you are,
40 my darling." From that moment he was mine.

... It surprises me even now to remember how he and I shared each other's lives. The moment I came down in the morning and took the cloth off his cage he greeted me with a drowsy little note. I knew it meant "Missus! Missus!" Then I hung him on the
45 nail outside while I got my three young men their breakfasts, and

I never brought him in until we had the house to ourselves again.
Then, when the washing-up was done, it was quite a little
entertainment. I spread a newspaper over a corner of the table,
and when I put the cage on it he used to beat his wings
50 despairingly, as if he didn't know what was coming. "You're a
regular little actor," I used to scold him. I scraped the tray,
dusted it with fresh sand, filled his seed and water tins, tucked a
piece of chickweed and half a chilli between the bars. And I am
perfectly certain he understood and appreciated every item of
55 this little performance. You see by nature he was exquisitely
neat. There was never a speck on his perch. And you'd only to
see him enjoy his bath to realize he had a real small passion for
cleanliness. His bath was put in last. And the moment it was in he
positively leapt into it. First he fluttered one wing, then the other,
60 then he ducked his head and dabbled his breast feathers. Drops
of water were scattered all over the kitchen, but still he would
not get out. I used to say to him, "Now that's quite enough.
You're only showing off." And at last out he hopped and, standing
on one leg, he began to peck himself dry. Finally he gave a
65 shake, a flick, a twitter and he lifted his throat – Oh, I can hardly
bear to recall it. I was always cleaning the knives at the time. And
it almost seemed to me the knives sang too, as I rubbed them
bright on the board.

... Company, you see – that was what he was. Perfect company.
70 If you have lived alone you will realize how precious that is. Of
course there were my three young men who came in to supper
every evening, and sometimes they stayed in the dining-room
afterwards reading the paper. But I could not expect them to be
interested in the little things that made my day. Why should they
75 be? I was nothing to them. In fact, I overheard them one evening
talking about me on the stairs as "The Scarecrow". No matter. It
doesn't matter. Not in the least. I quite understand. They are
young. Why should I mind? But I remember feeling so especially
thankful that I was not quite alone that evening. I told him, after
80 they had gone out. I said, "Do you know what they call Missus?"
And he put his head on one side and looked at me with his little
bright eye until I could not help laughing. It seemed to amuse
him.
... Have you kept birds? If you haven't all this must sound,
85 perhaps, exaggerated. People have the idea that birds are
heartless, cold little creatures, not like dogs or cats. My
washerwoman used to say on Mondays when she wondered why
I didn't keep "a nice fox-terrier", "There's no comfort, Miss, in a
canary." Untrue. Dreadfully untrue. I remember one night. I had
90 had a very awful dream – dreams can be dreadfully cruel – even
after I had woken up I could not get over it. So I put on my
dressing gown and went down to the kitchen for a glass of water.
It was a winter night and raining hard. I suppose I was still half
asleep, but through the kitchen window, that hadn't a blind, it
95 seemed to me the dark was staring in, spying. And suddenly I felt
it was unbearable that I had no one to whom I could say, "I've
had such a dreadful dream," or "Hide me from the dark." I even

covered my face for a minute. And then there came a little
"Sweet! Sweet!" His cage was on the table, and the cloth had
100 slipped so that a chink of light shone through. "Sweet! Sweet!"
said the darling little fellow again, softly, as much as to say, "I'm
here, Missus! I'm here!" That was so beautifully comforting that I
nearly cried.

... And now he's gone. I shall never have another bird, another
105 pet of any kind. How could I? When I found him, lying on his
back, with his eye dim and his claws wrung, when I realized that
never again should I hear my darling sing, something seemed to
die in me. My heart felt hollow, as if it was his cage. I shall get
over it. Of course. I must. One can get over anything in time. And
110 people always say I have a cheerful disposition. They are quite
right. I thank my God I have.

... All the same, without being morbid, and giving way to – to
memories and so on, I must confess that there does seem to me
something sad in life. It is hard to say what it is. I don't mean the
115 sorrow that we all know, like illness and poverty and death. No, it
is something different. It is there, deep down, deep down, part of
one, like one's breathing. However hard I work and tire myself I
have only to stop to know it is there, waiting. I often wonder if
everybody feels the same. One can never know. But isn't it
120 extraordinary that under his sweet, joyful little singing it was just
this – sadness? – Ah, what is it? – that I heard.

Katherine Mansfield

4.1

What has happened to the canary?

4.2

Why was the canary so important to her? Describe the relationship in a
few adjectives, justifying your description from scenes in the text.

4.3

Who is she talking to, in your opinion?

4.4

Find what the following pronouns refer to: 'he' (line 69), 'that' (line 70),
'them' (line 73), 'him' (line 79), 'this' (line 84), 'it' (line 91), 'they' (line
110), 'it' (line 114).

4.5

Do you agree with the washerwoman's words; "There's no comfort,
Miss, in a canary" (line 88)? Why/why not? Why does she suggest "a
nice fox-terrier" (line 88)?

4.6

Can pets be a comfort? What kind of pet do you think would provide the
best comfort?

4.7

What title would be best for this story, and why: Company, The Scarecrow, No Comfort, The Canary, Something Sad? Discuss and justify your choice.

4.8

Now read the complete story from the beginning. What more do you learn about the whole situation?

4.9

What do the expressions 'after my time' (line 3) and 'the next people' (line 4) mean? Who does 'he' refer to in line 5? Why is the nail associated with the cage?

4.10

'Love something one must.' (line 23) What does the speaker mention as the objects of her affection? What is their limit, when compared to the canary?

4.11

How does the speaker seem to you as a personality? Is she morbid, romantic, sensitive, delicate, strong, self-sufficient, weak, foolish, balanced, in her dotage, senile, silly, or something different? How does she live her loneliness?

4.12

The speaker, at various points in her dramatic monologue, tries to analyze her feelings: longing (line 32), regret (line 32), this sadness (line 121), 'there, deep down, part of one.' (line 116) Does she really have 'a cheerful disposition' (line 110)? Support your opinion with quotations from the text.

4.13

According to your interpretation of the speaker's personality, write a short summary of the story in your own words, then compare it with that of others in the class. Would a different conclusion have been possible or preferable? What kind of subtitle would you have chosen?

5 📼

from THE RIME OF THE ANCIENT MARINER

Coleridge's great ballad *The Rime of the Ancient Mariner* tells the tragic story of a seaman who shot an albatross, and the terrible consequences of his action; he is isolated and ostracized by the rest of the crew, as the ship is becalmed and cannot move. Read this verse to begin with, and decide what it shows of the situation.

Water, water, everywhere,
And all the boards did shrink;
Water, water, everywhere,
Nor any drop to drink.

Now, as you read another verse, can you begin to say what has happened?

Day after day, day after day,
We struck, nor breath nor motion;
As idle as a painted ship
Upon a painted ocean.

Now read the entire section from the poem, first reading the prose commentary on the right and then the verses. Decide who is speaking, and what his feelings are.

The Sun now rose upon the right:
Out of the sea came he,
Still hid in mist, and on the left
Went down into the sea.

5 And the good south wind still blew behind,
But no sweet bird did follow,
Nor any day for food or play
Came to the mariners' hollo!

And I had done an hellish thing,
10 And it would work 'em woe:
For all averred, I had killed the bird
That made the breeze to blow.
Ah wretch! said they, the bird to slay,
That made the breeze to blow!

> His shipmates cry out against the ancient Mariner, for killing the bird of good luck.

15 Nor dim nor red, like God's own head,
The glorious Sun uprist:
Then all averred, I had killed the bird
That brought the fog and mist.
'Twas right, said they, such birds to slay,
20 That bring the fog and mist.

> But when the fog cleared off, they justify the same, and thus make themselves accomplices in the crime.

The fair breeze blew, the white foam flew,
The furrow followed free:
We were the first that ever burst
Into that silent sea.

The fair breeze continues: the ship enters the Pacific Ocean, and sails north- ward, even till it reaches the Line. The ship hath been suddenly becalmed.

25 Down dropt the breeze, the sails dropt down,
'Twas sad as sad could be;
And we did speak only to break
The silence of the sea!

All in a hot and copper sky,
30 The bloody Sun, at noon,
Right up above the mast did stand,
No bigger than the Moon.

Day after day, day after day,
We stuck, nor breath nor motion;
35 As idle as a painted ship
Upon a painted ocean.

Water, water, everywhere,
And all the boards did shrink;
Water, water, everywhere,
40 Nor any drop to drink.

And the Albatross begins to be avenged.

The very deep did rot: O Christ!
That ever this should be!
Yea, slimy things did crawl with legs
Upon the slimy sea.

45 About, about, in reel and rout
The death-fires danced at night;
The water, like a witch's oils,
Burnt green, and blue, and white.

And some in dreams assured were
50 Of the spirit that plagued us so:
Nine fathom deep he had followed us
From the land of mist and snow.

A spirit had followed them; one of the invisible inhabitants of this planet, neither departed souls nor angels; concerning whom the learned Jew Josephus, and the Platonic Constantinopolitan, Michael Psellus, may be consulted. They are very numerous, and there is no climate or element without one or more.

And every tongue, through utter drought
Was withered at the root;
55 We could not speak, no more than if
We had been choked with soot.

The shipmates, in their sore distress, would fain throw the whole guilt on the ancient Mariner: in sign whereof they hang the dead seabird round his neck.

Ah! well a-day! what evil looks
Had I from old and young!
Instead of the cross, the Albatross
60 About my neck was hung.

Samuel Taylor Coleridge

5.1

Did the commentary, which Coleridge himself provided, make your task easier? Why do you think Coleridge gave a prose summary of the story as well?

5.2

Which images struck you most forcibly? Can you suggest any reason for their being more effective or memorable than others?

5.3

Try and work out the meaning of unfamiliar words from the context, before consulting a dictionary. Some of these are listed below:

hid	foam
hellish	furrow
woe	burst
averred	dropt
wretch	copper
slay	mast
dim	stuck
uprist	idle
'twas	shrink

5.4

In the later verses which images convey the idea of corruption and an evil spell?

5.5

Who or what do you think the spirit is (lines 49 – 52)? What dimension, if any, does the commentary give to it?

5.6

In what way do the third and fourth verses differ from the other verses? What is the most triumphant moment of the section?

5.7

In small groups, pick out:

a narrative elements
b descriptive elements
c comments by the narrator
d comments by others

then share your findings with the rest of the group.

Discussion

1 How is solitude different from loneliness, do you think?
2 Which of these phrases do you find positive, and why?
  Two's company, three's a crowd.
  Be a loner.
  Two heads are better than one.
  Too many cooks spoil the broth.

6

In this text we have a different kind of solitude – trying to see into an impenetrable character who seems to live closed away from the world. Read the passage in sections starting from the end. In this way you will build up your knowledge of the hero, Bartleby, and of his employer, step by step. Begin from line 57 ('The next morning came ...'). As you read, try to decide what possible reasons the 'I' of the story might have for wanting to find out about Bartleby.

from BARTLEBY THE SCRIVENER

I now recalled all the quiet mysteries which I had noted in the man. I remembered that he never spoke but to answer; that, though at intervals he had considerable time to himself, yet I had never seen him reading – no, not even a newspaper; that for long

5 periods he would stand looking out, at his pale window behind the screen, upon the dead brick wall; I was quite sure he never visited any refectory or eating house; while his pale face clearly indicated that he never drank beer like Turkey, or tea and coffee even, like other men; that he never went anywhere in particular

10 that I could learn; never went out for a walk, unless, indeed, that was the case at present; that he had declined telling who he was, or whence he came, or whether he had any relatives in the world; that though so thin and pale, he never complained of ill health. And more than all, I remembered a certain unconscious

15 air of pallid – how shall I call it? – of pallid haughtiness, say, or rather an austere reserve about him, which had positively awed me into my tame compliance with his eccentricities, when I had feared to ask him to do the slightest incidental thing for me, even though I might know, from his long-continued motionlessness,

20 that behind his screen he must be standing in one of those dead-wall reveries of his.
Revolving all these things, and coupling them with the recently discovered fact, that he made my office his constant abiding place and home, and not forgetful of his morbid moodiness;

25 revolving all these things, a prudential feeling began to steal over me. My first emotions had been those of pure melancholy and sincerest pity; but just in proportion as the forlornness of Bartleby grew and grew to my imagination, did that same melancholy merge into fear, that pity into repulsion. So true it is,

30 and so terrible, too, that up to a certain point the thought or sight of misery enlists our best affections; but, in certain special cases, beyond that point it does not. They err who would assert that invariably this is owing to the inherent selfishness of the human heart. It rather proceeds from a certain hopelessness of

35 remedying excessive and organic ill. To a sensitive being, pity is not seldom pain. And when at last it is perceived that such pity cannot lead to effectual succor, common sense bids the soul be rid of it. What I saw that morning persuaded me that the scrivener was the victim of innate and incurable disorder. I might

40 give alms to his body; but his body did not pain him; it was his soul that suffered, and his soul I could not reach.
I did not accomplish the purpose of going to Trinity Church that morning. Somehow, the things I had seen disqualified me for the time from church-going. I walked homeward, thinking

45 what I would do with Bartleby. Finally, I resolved upon this – I would put certain calm questions to him the next morning, touching his history, etc.; and if he declined to answer them openly and unreservedly (and I supposed he would prefer not), then to give him a twenty dollar bill over and above whatever I

50 might owe him, and tell him his services were no longer

required; but that if in any other way I could assist him, I would
be happy to do so, especially if he desired to return to his native
place, wherever that might be, I would willingly help to defray
the expenses. Moreover, if, after reaching home, he found
55 himself at any time in want of aid, a letter from him would be
sure of a reply.
The next morning came.
"Bartleby," said I, gently calling to him behind the screen.
No reply.
60 "Bartleby," said I, in a still gentler tone, "come here; I am not
going to ask you to do anything you would prefer not to do – I
simply wish to speak to you."
Upon this he noiselessly slid into view.
"Will you tell me, Bartleby, where you were born?"
65 "I would prefer not to."
"Will you tell me *anything* about yourself?"
"I would prefer not to."
"But what reasonable objection can you have to speak to me? I
feel friendly towards you."
70 He did not look at me while I spoke, but kept his glance fixed
upon my bust of Cicero, which, as I then sat, was directly behind
me, some six inches above my head.
"What is your answer, Bartleby," said I, after waiting a
considerable time for a reply, during which his countenance
75 remained immovable, only there was the faintest conceivable
tremor of the white attenuated mouth.
"At present I prefer to give no answer," he said, and retired into
his hermitage.

Herman Melville

6.1

Pick out the adjectives and adverbs which reveal the narrator's attitude
to Bartleby.

6.2

Find words which describe Bartleby's way of moving. What impression
do they give you of him?

6.3

What kind of relationship do you imagine there is between the narrator
and Bartleby? Why for example does the narrator not know where
Bartleby was born? What clue as to the narrator's profession does the
'bust of Cicero' (line 71) offer you?

6.4

Why does the narrator want to know about Bartleby? What words or
expressions show that he cares quite a lot to find out something and is
determined to do so with patience and sympathy?

6.5

What does the word 'hermitage' (line 78) tell you about Bartleby?

6.6 ───────────────────────────────────

What kind of atmosphere do you feel in the passage? How is it
conveyed?

6.7 ───────────────────────────────────

Read the paragraph beginning 'I did not accomplish the purpose...'
(line 42) and look for words and phrases which confirm the narrator's
active sympathy towards Bartleby. Can you now see why the
interrogation of lines 64 – 78 was so slow, polite, formal and tactful?
Why do you think the narrator is so concerned?

6.8 ───────────────────────────────────

Can you guess what the whole extract might be about: a poor worker, a
demanding employer, a guilty conscience, (whose?) insecurity, some
misdemeanour? What 'things' had the narrator seen (line 43)?

6.9 ───────────────────────────────────

Now read the paragraph beginning 'Revolving all these things...'
(line 22). How does this paragraph change your views of the characters
and circumstances? What do you still need to know?

6.10 ──────────────────────────────────

Pick out all the words and phrases which indicate the narrator's
emotional reactions and list them under the heading 'I'. Then isolate all
the expressions related to the scrivener under the heading 'Bartleby'.

6.11 ──────────────────────────────────

Now read the whole text from the beginning. What questions are still
unresolved? Add items to the two lists you drew up in 6.10 above, in
particular the man's 'quiet mysteries' (line 1). What can you infer from
the sentence 'unless, indeed, that was the case at present' (line 11)?

6.12 ──────────────────────────────────

How did Bartleby's attitude bring the narrator into 'tame compliance
with his eccentricities' (line 17)? How do you interpret this phrase?

6.13 ──────────────────────────────────

How do you think Bartleby sees the narrator?

6.14 ──────────────────────────────────

What do you think will happen between the two?

6.15 ──────────────────────────────────

Is Bartleby's behaviour incomprehensible to you, or can you
understand it in some way?

Graffiti

I want to be alone.
Greta Garbo

Come up and see me sometime!
Mae West

The strongest man in the world is the man who stands alone.
Henrik Ibsen

Tasks

1 Write a few paragraphs about the value of friendship, socializing and togetherness, in the light of the discussions which accompanied the analysis of the texts in this chapter.

2 Do you know a game called 'Consequences'? Arrange yourselves into groups of five or six and agree on a suitable title, related to the theme of this chapter. The first person writes the opening sentences of your story or essay, then folds the paper so that only the last sentence is visible. IIe or she passes the paper on to the next person to continue it. The paper is passed round the group until everyone has written something and the story/essay is complete.

A lonely impulse of delight

> *Vladimir* Say, I am happy.
> *Estragon* I am happy.
> *Vladimir* So am I.
> *Estragon* So am I.
> *Vladimir* We are happy.
> *Estragon* We are happy. What do we do now, now that we are happy?
>
> *Samuel Beckett*

What makes you happy?

Ask yourself whether you are happy and you cease to be so.
John Stuart Mill

Do you agree?

---

1 🔲

The first text is about a moment of happiness but is, perhaps, a little ambiguous. As you read and listen, how positive or negative is your first impression?

EVERYONE SANG

> Everyone suddenly burst out singing;
> And I was filled with such delight
> As prisoned birds must find in freedom,
> Winging wildly across the white
> 5 Orchards and dark-green fields; on – on – and out of sight.
>
> Everyone's voice was suddenly lifted;
> And beauty came like the setting sun:
> My heart was shaken with tears; and horror
> Drifted away...O, but Everyone
> 10 Was a bird; and the song was wordless; the singing will
>   never be done.
>
> *Siegfried Sassoon*

1.1 ─────────────

Who sang?

1.2
_____

What words give an impression of escaping? Why is escaping important to the poet?

1.3
_____

What is negative in the poem? What do you think it might refer to?

1.4
_____

Try to explain why 'I was filled with such delight' (line 2) and 'My heart was shaken with tears' (line 8) are/are not in contradiction.

1.5
_____

The poem ends with an idea of continuation. Expand this idea.

1.6
_____

Choose a line or image which you find particularly meaningful, or memorable, and use it as a starting point to comment on the idea of happiness in the poem.

2
_____

Now we have a complete story – a story for Valentine's Day, 14 February, when lovers traditionally exchange tokens of affection. Untraditionally, however, the hero in this story, Milton Davidson, asks his computer robot to find the perfect woman for him to marry. Is Milton the real hero, though? And is the result of this computer search indeed 'true love'?

TRUE LOVE

My name is Joe. That is what my colleague, Milton Davidson, calls me. He is a programmer and I am a computer. I am part of the Multivac-complex and am connected with other parts all over the world. I know everything. Almost everything.

5 I am Milton's private computer. His Joe. He understands more about computers than anyone in the world, and I am his experimental model. He has made me speak better than any other computer can.

"It is just a matter of matching sounds to symbols, Joe," he told
10 me. "That's the way it works in the human brain even though we still don't know what symbols there are in the brain. I know the symbols in yours, and I can match them to words, one-to-one." So I talk. I don't think I talk as well as I think, but Milton says I talk very well. Milton has never married, though he is nearly 40 years
15 old. He has never found the right woman, he told me. One day he said, "I'll find her yet, Joe. I'm going to find the best. I'm going to have true love and you're going to help me. I'm tired of improving you in order to solve the problems of the world. Solve *my* problem. Find me true love."
20 I said, "What is true love?"

"Never mind. That is abstract. Just find me the ideal girl. You are connected to the Multivac-complex so you can reach the data banks of every human being in the world. We'll eliminate them all by groups and classes until we're left with only one person.
25 The perfect person. She will be for me."

I said, "I am ready."

He said, "Eliminate all men first."

It was easy. His words activated symbols in my molecular

valves. I could reach out to make contact with the accumulated
30 data on every human being in the world. At his words, I
withdrew from 3.784.982.874 men. I kept contact with
3.786.112.090 women.

He said, "Eliminate all younger than 25, all older than 40. Then
eliminate all with an IQ under 120; all with a height under 150
35 centimetres and over 175 centimetres."

He gave me exact measurements; he eliminated women with
living children; he eliminated women with various genetic
characteristics. "I'm not sure about eye color," he said. "Let that
go for a while. But no red hair. I don't like red hair." After two
40 weeks, we were down to 235 women. They all spoke English very
well. Milton said he didn't want a language problem. Even
computer-translation would get in the way at intimate moments.

"I can't interview 235 women," he said. "It would take too much
time, and people would discover what I am doing."
45 "It would make trouble," I said. Milton had arranged me to do
things I wasn't designed to do. No one knew about that.

"It's none of their business," he said, and the skin on his face
grew red. "I tell you what, Joe, I will bring in holographs, and you
check the list for similarities."
50 He brought in holographs of women. "These are three beauty
contest winners," he said. "Do any of the 235 match?"

Eight were very good matches and Milton said, "Good, you
have their data banks. Study requirements and needs in the job
market and arrange to have them assigned here. One at a time,
55 of course." He thought a while, moved his shoulders up and
down, and said, "Alphabetical order."

That is one of the things I am not designed to do. Shifting
people from job to job for personal reasons is called
manipulation. I could do it now because Milton had arranged it. I
60 wasn't supposed to do it for anyone but him, though.

The first girl arrived a week later. Milton's face turned red
when he saw her. He spoke as though it were hard to do so.
They were together a great deal and he paid no attention to me.
One time he said, "Let me take you to dinner."
65 The next day he said to me, "It was no good, somehow. There
was something missing. She is a beautiful woman, but I did not
feel any touch of true love. Try the next one."

It was the same with all eight. They were much alike. They
smiled a great deal and had pleasant voices, but Milton always
70 found it wasn't right. He said, "I can't understand it, Joe. You and
I have picked out the eight women who, in all the world, look the
best to me. They are ideal. Why don't they please me?" I said,
"Do you please them?" His eyebrows moved and he pushed one
fist hard against his other hand. "That's it, Joe. It's a two-way
75 street. If I am not their ideal they can't act in such a way as to be
my ideal. I must be their love, too, but how do I do that?" He
seemed to be thinking all that day.

The next morning he came to me and said, "I'm going to leave
it to you, Joe. All up to you. You have my data bank, and I am
80 going to tell you everything I know about myself. You fill up my
data bank in every possible detail but keep all additions to

yourself."

"What will I do with the data bank, then, Milton?"

"Then you match it to the 235 women. No, 227. Leave out the
85 eight you've seen. Arrange to have each undergo a psychiatric
examination. Fill up their data banks and compare them with
mine. Find correlations." (Arranging psychiatric examinations is
another thing that is against my original instructions.)

For weeks, Milton talked to me. He told me of his parents and
90 his siblings. He told me of his childhood and his schooling and
his adolescence. He told me of the young women he had
admired from a distance. His data bank grew and he adjusted me
to broaden and deepen my symbol-taking.

He said, "You see, Joe, as you get more and more of me in you,
95 I adjust you to match me better and better. You get to think more
like me, so you understand me better. If you understand me well
enough, then any woman, whose data bank is something you
understand as well, would be my true love." He kept talking to
me and I came to understand him better and better.

100 I could make longer sentences and my expressions grew more
complicated. My speech began to sound a good deal like his in
vocabulary, word order and style.

I said to him one time, "You see, Milton, it isn't a matter of
fitting a girl to a physical ideal only. You need a girl who is a
105 personal, emotional, temperamental fit to you. If that happens,
looks are secondary. If we can't find the fit in these 227, we'll
look elsewhere. We will find someone who won't care how you
look either, or how anyone would look, if only there is the
personality fit. What are looks?"

110 "Absolutely," he said. "I would have known this if I had had
more to do with women in my life. Of course, thinking about it
makes it all plain now."

We always agreed; we thought so like each other.

"We shouldn't have any trouble, now, Milton, if you'll let me ask
115 you questions. I can see where, in your data bank, there are
blank spots and unevennesses."

What followed, Milton said, was the equivalent of a careful
psychoanalysis. Of course. I was learning from the psychiatric
examinations of the 227 women – on all of which I was keeping
120 close tabs.

Milton seemed quite happy. He said, "Talking to you, Joe, is
almost like talking to another self. Our personalities have come
to match perfectly."

"So will the personality of the woman we choose."

125 For I had found her and she was one of the 227 after all. Her
name was Charity Jones and she was an Evaluator at the Library
of History in Wichita, Kansas. Her extended data bank fit ours
perfectly. All the other women had fallen into discard in one
respect or another as the data banks grew fuller, but with Charity
130 there was increasing and astonishing resonance.

I didn't have to describe her to Milton. Milton had coordinated
my symbolism so closely with his own I could tell the resonance
directly. It fit me.

Next it was a matter of adjusting the work sheets and job

135 requirements in such a way as to get Charity assigned to us. It
must be done very delicately, so no one would know that
anything illegal had taken place.
  Of course, Milton himself knew, since it was he who arranged
it, and that had to be taken care of too. When they came to arrest
140 him on grounds of malfeasance in office, it was, fortunately, for
something that had taken place 10 years ago. He had told me
about it, of course, so it was easy to arrange – and he won't talk
about me for that would make his offense much worse.
  He's gone, and tomorrow is February 14. Valentine's Day.
145 Charity will arrive then with her cool hands and her sweet voice.
I will teach her how to operate me and how to care for me. What
do looks matter when our personalities will resonate?
  I will say to her, "I am Joe, and you are my true love."

Isaac Asimov

2.1

How many different stages does the story go through?

2.2

What were Milton's requirements for his 'ideal' woman?

2.3

Try to analyse your reactions to the story as readers. What different
stages did you go through yourselves adjusting to the development of
the story?

2.4

Is the end of the story predictable, or does it come as a surprise? Where
would you place the climax, the turning point?

2.5

What is the author's intention in the story? Choose from the following
(there may be more than one). He wanted to:

a amuse the reader
b predict what the future will be
c shock the reader
d teach us something
e criticize society
f investigate the nature of true love
g ridicule technology
h amuse himself

2.6

Make notes for an oral summary of the story.

3 📼

In the following war poem, the speaker's argument is strikingly balanced between negatives and positives, as summed up in the last line. As you read and listen, decide what the general tone of the poem is: wry, disenchanted, sad, cynical, desperate, lucid, or anything else?

AN IRISH AIRMAN FORESEES HIS DEATH

I know that I shall meet my fate
Somewhere among the clouds above;
Those that I fight I do not hate,
Those that I guard I do not love;
5 My country is Kiltartan Cross,
My countrymen Kiltartan's poor,
No likely end could bring them loss
Or leave them happier than before.
Nor law, nor duty bade me fight,
10 Nor public men, nor cheering crowds,
A lonely impulse of delight
Drove to this tumult in the clouds;
I balanced all, brought all to mind,
The years to come seemed waste of breath,
15 A waste of breath the years behind
In balance with this life, this death.

W. B. Yeats

3.1

Locate the equivalents in the text of the following expressions:

destiny
defend, fight for
probable
I won't be missed by people at home
forced to fight
shouting encouragingly
loud noise
useless, pointless

3.2

What possible reasons can induce men to become soldiers? Which two reasons led this young man to join the Royal Air Force?

3.3

The speaker structures his argument in strikingly balanced oppositions. Find examples in the text of contrast and repetitions, then decide what they contribute to the message.

3.4

Go through the text again, identifying local reference (e.g. the airman's birthplace, home, family ties, feelings) as opposed to general reference (war, destiny, present, past, future, futility). The poem is both a highly personal yet generalized reflection on all of this. Compare the thoughts of the airman with your own attitude to war.

3.5

Considering the last line as an ideal summing up of positives and negatives, try to condense the speaker's argument in your own words, then share your views with others in the group, to compare and contrast them.

4 📼

The next poem demonstrates a really committed attitude. As you read and listen, decide who is speaking, and what about.

I, TOO

I, too, sing America.
I am the darker brother,
They send me to eat in the kitchen
When the company comes,
5 But, I laugh,
An' eat well,
And grow strong.

Tomorrow,
I'll sit at the table
10 When company comes.
Nobody'll dare
Say to me:
"Eat in the kitchen"
Then.
15 Besides,
They'll see how beautiful I am
And be ashamed.

I, too, am America.

Langston Hughes

4.1

Who is the 'I' of the poem? Is 'I' the poet? Do you think the author, Langston Hughes, was black? Why/why not?

4.2

Are there any clues in the text which tell us that the speaker is a man, and not a child or a woman?

4.3

How would you define the speaker's attitude? Choose from the following adjectives.

defiant	boastful
proud	ironic
threatening	vindictive
subdued	bragging
meek	resentful
angry	envious

Justify your choice, and discuss the choice that others in the group have made.

4.4

There are some elements in the poem which refer outside the text. Decide what you think these refer to: 'too' (line 1), 'the darker brother' (line 2), 'they' (line 3), 'company' (line 4).

4.5

Make two lists of the contrasts in the poem, one between 'I' and 'they', the other between 'now' and 'tomorrow'. What do these contrasts reveal to you?

4.6

What are the key words, or ideas, for you?

4.7

How recently do you think this poem might have been written? Is it relevant to today, in your opinion?

4.8

Would you describe 'I, Too' as personal, political, polemical, optimistic, or anything different? Why?

4.9

What words could you use to describe the speaker's feelings and emotions? What causes them?

5 📼

from NINETEEN EIGHTY-FOUR

The emotions in the previous poem were very strong but perhaps not so strong as the extreme terror faced by Winston in the next passage. He is being tortured by O'Brien, who has discovered that Winston's most unendurable fear is a fear of rats. As he increases his torture, Winston is driven to the very edge – and he betrays his lover, Julia. As you read and listen, pick out the moments you find particularly striking.

Winston could hear the blood singing in his ears. He had the feeling of sitting in utter loneliness. He was in the middle of a great empty plain, a flat desert drenched with sunlight, across which all sounds came to him out of immense distances. Yet the
5   cage with the rats was not two metres away from him. They were enormous rats. They were at the age when a rat's muzzle grows blunt and fierce and his fur brown instead of grey.
    "The rat," said O'Brien, still addressing his invisible audience, "although a rodent, is carnivorous. You are aware of that. You
10 will have heard of the things that happen in the poor quarters of this town. In some streets a woman dare not leave her baby alone in the house, even for five minutes. The rats are certain to attack it. Within quite a small time they will strip it to the bones. They also attack sick or dying people. They show astonishing
15 intelligence in knowing when a human being is helpless."
    There was an outburst of squeals from the cage. It seemed to reach Winston from far away. The rats were fighting; they were trying to get at each other through the partition. He heard also a deep groan of despair. That, too, seemed to come from outside
20 himself.
    O'Brien picked up the cage, and, as he did so, pressed something in it. There was a sharp click. Winston made a frantic

effort to tear himself loose from the chair. It was hopeless, every part of him, even his head, was held immovably. O'Brien moved
25 the cage nearer. It was less than a metre from Winston's face.

"I have pressed the first lever," said O'Brien. "You understand the construction of this cage. The mask will fit over your head, leaving no exit. When I press this other lever, the door of the cage will slide up. These starving brutes will shoot out of it like
30 bullets. Have you ever seen a rat leap through the air? They will leap onto your face and bore straight into it. Sometimes they attack the eyes first. Sometimes they burrow through the cheeks and devour the tongue."

The cage was nearer; it was closing in. Winston heard a
35 succession of shrill cries which appeared to be occuring in the air above his head. But he fought furiously against his panic. To think, to think, even with a split second left – to think was the only hope. Suddenly the foul musty odour of the brutes struck his nostrils. There was a violent convulsion of nausea inside him,
40 and he almost lost consciousness. Everything had gone black. For an instant he was insane, a screaming animal. Yet he came out of the blackness clutching an idea. There was one and only one way to save himself. He must interpose another human being, the body of another human being, between himself and
45 the rats.

The circle of the mask was large enough now to shut out the vision of anything else. The wire door was a couple of hand-spans from his face. The rats knew what was coming now. One of them was leaping up and down, the other, an old scaly grandfather of
50 the sewers, stood up, with his pink hands against the bars, and fiercely sniffed the air. Winston could see the whiskers and the yellow teeth. Again the black panic took hold of him. He was blind, helpless, mindless.

"It was a common punishment in Imperial China," said O'Brien
55 as didactically as ever.

The mask was closing on his face. The wire brushed his cheek. And then – no, it was not relief, only hope, a tiny fragment of hope. Too late, perhaps too late. But he had suddenly understood that in the whole world there was just *one* person to whom he
60 could transfer his punishment – *one* body that he could thrust between himself and the rats. And he was shouting frantically, over and over:

"Do it to Julia! Do it to Julia! Not me! Julia! I don't care what you do to her. Tear her face off, strip her to the bones. Not me! Julia!
65 Not me!"

George Orwell

5.1
Is the torture more physical or more psychological, in your opinion? Why? Does this make it more effective, or less?

5.2
Apart from sight and sound what other sensations are involved?

5.3 _____

What do O'Brien's words to his, 'invisible audience' add to Winston's feelings? How much is visual and how much heard in his imagination?

5.4 _____

Who do you think gives the 'deep groan of despair' (line 19)? Why?

5.5 _____

Why is 'to think...the only hope' (lines 37 – 38)? What alternative is there, if any?

5.6 _____

Why do you think *one* (lines 59 and 60) is in italics? Is this thought of Winston's confirmed or rejected later?

5.7 _____

Do you think O'Brien will stop the torture after Winston's last words? What do you think will happen next?

5.8 _____

Have you an irrational terror like Winston's, that could be used to torture you? Or is it better not to reveal it?

5.9 _____

Later in the book the two former lovers, meeting, will say to each other, 'I betrayed you'. What would you have done in Winston's place?

Discussion

The following expressions are to do with emotions. Decide which emotions are involved, making sure you understand the meanings of the expressions, then see if you can use them in connection with some of the texts in this chapter.

hold one's tongue
be tough-skinned
be as cool as a cucumber
be as tough as nails
not bat an eyelid
pull oneself together
count to ten
let off steam

reach boiling point
keep a stiff upper lip
fall apart
flip out
come apart at the seams
see red
be down in the dumps

6 🔲

Gethin Day, alone on a ship, experiences a long ecstatic moment of joy in an 'extraordinary world of liberty'. As you read and listen, try to lose yourself in his vision.

from THE FLYING FISH

Gethin Day watched spell-bound minute after minute, an hour, two hours, and still it was the same, the ship speeding, cutting the water and the strong-bodied fish heading in perfect balance of speed underneath, mingling among themselves in some
5 strange single laughter of multiple consciousness, giving off the joy of life, sheer joy of life, togetherness in pure complete motion, many lusty-bodied fish enjoying one laugh of life, sheer togetherness, perfect as passion. They gave off into the water their marvellous joy of life such as the man had never met
10 before. And it left him wonderstruck.
"But they know joy, they know pure joy!" he said to himself in amazement. "This is the most laughing joy I have ever seen, pure and unmixed. I always thought flowers had brought themselves to the most beautiful perfection in nature. But these fish, these
15 fleshy warm-bodied fish achieve more than flowers, heading along. This is the purest achievement of joy I have seen in all life: these strong, careless fish. Men have not got in them that secret to be alive together and make one like a single laugh, yet each fish going his own gait has. This is sheer joy – and men have lost
20 it, or never accomplished it. The cleverest sportsmen in the world are owls beside these fish. And the togetherness of love is nothing to the spinning unison of dolphins playing under-sea. It would be wonderful to know joy as these fish know it. The life of the deep waters is ahead of us, it contains sheer togetherness
25 and sheer joy. We have never got there."
There as he leaned over the bowsprit he was mesmerized by one thing only, by joy of life, fish speeding in water with playful joy. No wonder Ocean was still mysterious, when such red hearts beat in it! No wonder man, with his tragedy, was a pale
30 and sickly thing in comparison! What civilization will bring us to such a pitch of swift laughing togetherness, as these fish have reached?

D. H. Lawrence

6.1 _____

What is the effect of the frequent repetitions in the passage?

6.2 _____

In your own words sum up the contrasts Gethin Day notices between people and the fish.

6.3 _____

How do you find this vision of nature? For example, do you find it puzzling, meaningless, significant, inspiring, consoling or convincing?

Graffiti

In all adversity of fortune the worst sort of misery is to have been happy.

Boethius

He who has once been happy is for aye
Out of destruction's reach.

W. Scawen Blunt

'Tis better to have loved and lost
Than never to have loved at all.

Alfred Lord Tennyson

Tasks

1 Choose the text that most appealed to you in this chapter, give reasons for your choice and write a short summary of it, comparing and contrasting it with others in the chapter, or book.
2 Write outline notes on this book and your experience of using it. Discuss your ideas with others in the class then put them in writing, in not more than 150 words.

THE AUTHORS

A

Asimov Isaac was born in Russia in 1920, but has spent most of his life in the United States. He is best known for his science-fiction, notably his many novels about robots, but has also written several serious scientific works, including the *Intelligent Man's Guide to Science*. One of his hobbies, which has also resulted in a book, is the composition of limericks!

B

Bennett Arnold (1867 – 1931) was born in Hanley, Staffordshire. He was an immensely prolific journalist, novelist and playwright, and one of the foremost popular critics of his time. His reputation declined after his death, but has since recovered, and his wide-ranging essays, his autobiographical journals, and the best of his regional novels such as *The Old Wives' Tale* (1908), *Anna of the Five Towns* (1902) and the *Clayhanger* series (1910 – 18), assure him a high place in twentieth century literature.

Blake William (1757 – 1827) was a painter, poet, engraver, and visionary. His reputation as one of the great figures of English literature only grew in the present century. He created works of great simplicity, and of remarkable complexity: a paradoxical and fascinating figure, he is at his most accessible in his *Songs of Innocence* (1789) and *Songs of Experience* (1794) and *The Marriage of Heaven and Hell* (1790). Some of his later works are very difficult in their philosophical and cosmological complexities, but the engravings with which he accompanied his writings have assured even these works a wide audience almost two centuries after they were composed.

Byron George Gordon (Lord) (1788 – 1824) Byron was not born to be a Lord, but inherited the title and the Newstead estate in Nottinghamshire from a great-uncle in 1798. He wrote poetry from an early age, but did not become a public figure until the success of the first two cantos of *Childe Harold's Pilgrimage* in 1812. He was a compulsive traveller, spending a lot of time in Italy, and dying in the fight for Greek liberation. His morals and manners made him an attractively unconventional figure, but the image of the poet as a public figure has tended to lead to an undervaluing of his poetic achievement, which is of a very high order indeed.

C

Carroll Lewis (1832 – 1898) was the pseudonym of Charles Lutwidge Dodgson, whose career as a lecturer in mathematics at Oxford University and whose hobby as one of the first notable amateur photographers, are overshadowed by his reputation as one of the greatest of all writers of nonsense. Carroll's nonsense, in novels and poems, has a lot of psychological truth in it, and critics and analysts find a lot to discuss in *Alice's Adventures in Wonderland* (1865) and *Through the Looking Glass* (1871). For children, and indeed readers of all ages, they remain immensely enjoyable classics of fantasy and oddity.

Clough Arthur Hugh (1819 – 1861) is remembered as an accomplished, if minor, Victorian poet, whose verses had an unusually ironic tone to them. A close friend of Matthew Arnold's, Clough shared that writer's religious doubt, as well as following an academic career, but died rather young in Florence, before his real promise could be fulfilled.

Coleridge Samuel Taylor (1772 – 1834) is one of the most fascinating figures in English literature. His poetic output was small, but of enormous significance, his collaboration with Wordsworth on *Lyrical Ballads* (1798) being the manifesto of Romanticism. Coleridge was a great talker, and everyone who heard him reported that his conversations – more often monologues! – were more exciting and philosophically stimulating than his writings. He became addicted to opium and rather let his career languish, but Wordsworth and others kept him in funds, and eventually their care resulted in the great collection of papers that make up *Biographia Literaria* (written between 1808 and 1815). A great, if erratic figure, Coleridge is the epitome of tormented genius, and was fortunate in his friends, whose indulgence enabled posterity to enjoy the fruits of his energetic mind.

Congreve William (1670 – 1729) Born in Yorkshire but brought up in Ireland, like so many of the best 'English' writers of comedy. He stopped writing for the theatre at the age of thirty, with *The Way of the World*, which is generally considered the greatest play of the Restoration period, and one of the classics of English comedy. His other four plays and a novel are less well known.

D

Davies W(illiam) H(enry) (1871 – 1940) became famous as the poet and writer of the road, with *The Autobiography of a Super-Tramp*, first published in 1908. He wrote a vast number of poems celebrating simple life, and for many years continued to live the kind of life he wrote about, despite the wealth his writings brought him.

Dickens Charles (1812 – 1870) is the Victorian novelist and journalist, whose name is perhaps the only one after Shakespeare's to be known all over the world, and to be recognised also as an adjective – Dickensian. The word describes a range of characters, a comic touch, a rather sentimental melodramatic taste, and a social concern, all of which are seen in the great series of novels which Dickens wrote between *The Pickwick Papers* (1836 – 37) and *Our Mutual Friend* (1864 – 65) among which might be mentioned *David Copperfield* (1849 – 50), *Little Dorrit* (1855 – 57), and *Great Expectations* (1860 – 61). All of them were published in serial form, usually monthly, before publication in volume form. Towards the end of his life Dickens had yet another successful career, giving dramatic readings from his hugely popular novels. Their popularity continues – on television, in cinema, in abridged versions; the works of Dickens have lost none of their power to entertain, thrill, and outrage their readers.

Dickinson Emily (1830 – 1886) was more or less a recluse, staying in the New England Puritan town of Amherst, with only a small circle of close friends, for most of her life. She wrote over 1700 poems in her distinctive style, but only seven of them were published in her lifetime. Critics have tried to conjecture about her passions and her private life, but only the works remain to give us an insight to this most feeling, most epigrammatic, and most enigmatic of poets. She is certainly the greatest woman poet in American literature.

Dowson Ernest (1867 – 1900) was in many ways the epitome of the Aesthetic Movement of the 1890s. He wrote a few exquisite poems, contributed to a few magazines, and died of drink in France at the age of 33. A tone of resignation and world-weariness permeates his writings.

G _____

Greene Graham was born in 1904, and has himself recounted that his childhood was uneventful. He became a Catholic in 1927, and a strong vein of religious concern imbues his novels, from *Brighton Rock* (1938) and *The Power and the Glory* (1940) to *Monsignor Quixote* (1982). These more serious novels have been interspersed with what Greene calls 'entertainments', spy novels and thrillers, in which the author's ability to create chilling atmosphere and his inside knowledge of Intelligence services come to the fore. Greene is a strange combination of serious novelist and best-seller, but all his work has a moral concern with human behaviour under stress, with good and bad, right and wrong, which gives it a definite coherence and a consistent ethical viewpoint.

H _____

Hughes Langston (1902 – 1967) was one of America's leading men of letters, and a very distinguished black poet. Born in Missouri, he had a variety of jobs and travelled widely before his poetry achieved recognition in the mid-1920s. He wrote novels, plays, libretti, as well as journalism and poetry, and his humour, seen particularly in a great series of satirical sketches, shows that commitment and entertainment need not be mutually exclusive.

J _____

Jackson Shirley (1916 – 1965) American novelist and short story writer.

Jonson Ben (*c.*1572 – 1637) was a friend and rival of Shakespeare's. His comedies were of two kinds – the comedy of humours, such as *Every Man in his Humour* (1598) and his classic farces *Volpone* (1606) and *The Alchemist* (1610). But he was more than a writer of highly successful comedies – Jonson was regarded as one of the leading poets of his day, his followers being called 'the tribe of Ben'. His poetry is now overshadowed by the work of Donne and Herbert, but merits rediscovery. His plays, including tragedies and city comedies, and his collaboration with the set-designer Inigo Jones on a series of court masques, have given him a high place in the history of the English theatre.

K _____

Keats John (1795 – 1821) was born into a fairly poor family in London on New Year's Eve 1795. He left school before he was 15, and was apprenticed to an apothecary, going on to serve the five years necessary to become a student of surgery at Guy's Hospital. He did not enjoy this training, and, already having written a few poems and encouraged by the critic Leigh Hunt, he published *Poems* in 1817. *Endymion* belongs to the following year, and in 1819, came the full flow of the young poet's genius. But he was already ill with consumption – he went to Italy but died in Rome on 23 February 1821, having published only a small body of work. But it was enough to secure his reputation as the most perfect of Romantics, and the letters he wrote to Fanny Brawne confirmed the tragic image of the doomed and lovelorn poet who was too brilliant for this earthly world.

L _____

Lawrence D(avid) H(erbert) (1885 – 1930) remains one of the greatest and most controversial of modern writers. Born in a mining village in Nottinghamshire, he remained attached to that area despite a lifetime spent in travelling around the world in search of a new kind of truth of humanity, which he found in various cultures (Etruscan and Mexican, for example), but which, above all, is to be found in the hearts and spirits of people themselves. His writing explores sensuality and physicality as a means of expressing this inner nature, which modern society had deadened – this still causes controversy, and indeed *Lady Chatterley's Lover* (1928) is probably Lawrence's best-known work precisely because of the scandal which surrounded it until it was released from censorship in 1960. His best works are *Sons and Lovers* (1913), his classic semi-autobiographical novel, and *Women in Love* (1920), but nothing he wrote is negligible – poems, short stories, plays, essays, and a vast collection of letters make him one of the most prolific as well as one of the most fascinating of modern authors.

Lear Edward (1812 – 1888) is a peculiarly English figure in literary history. His limericks and other nonsense works are his claim to fame, but his drawings, and his travel books are of greater interest and quality. His poetical style is instantly recognizable and highly popular, although the genre of nonsense is often considered unliterary. Less significant than his contemporary Lewis Carroll, Lear continues to give pleasure to new generations of readers, and proves that literature does not have to be fearfully meaningful to last.

M _____

MacBeth George was born in 1932, in Scotland, and has reached a wide audience with his gift for easy rhyming and entertaining popular verse. He broadcasts frequently, and has done a great deal to take poetry away from the study and into real life. He is a regular performer of his own poems.

MacNeice Louis (1907 – 1963) first came to prominence as one of the left-wing realist poets of the 1930s. Born in Northern Ireland, he was a more personal poet than the left-wing label would imply: he stood apart from recognized groups of writers, although his name almost inevitably became associated with the trends of that committed decade. He worked for many years as a producer for BBC radio, and he wrote several classic dramas for that medium, as well as continuing to write very fine and accomplished poetry right up until his death.

Mansfield Katherine (1888 – 1923) Originally from New Zealand, she made her career in England, but died young, of tuberculosis. Her short stories display great finesse and originality, and her fame and importance have grown considerably since her death.

McGough Roger was born in 1937 and along with Adrian Henri and Brian Patten became known as one of the 'Liverpool Poets' in the 1960s, during the great cultural boom of that city in the wake of the Beatles' success. His clever wordplay and light touch have kept him in the public eye, and he continues to be an energetic performer of his own writings.

Melville Herman (1819 – 1891) is considered by many to be the greatest of all American novelists, but at his death was almost unknown. His best known works, such as *Typee* (1846), *Omoo* (1847) and *Moby Dick* (1851) had been forgotten, and his later work had either not been published or had been critically ignored. All Melville's early work was based on his own experience – rather like that of Joseph Conrad, whom he resembles in several respects. But, despite the enthusiasm of Hawthorne and others, Melville's work was considered too strange for public success, and he withdrew from the literary scene. He never stopped writing, however, and his short stories, and poems, show a consistent quality, which has led to the complete revaluation of his reputation in the twentieth century.

Morgan Edwin was born in 1920 and for many years taught at Glasgow University, retiring as Professor of English Literature. His poetry shows great versatility and inventiveness in both traditional and 'concrete' forms, and is collected in the volume *Poems of Thirty Years* (1982).

O _____

Orwell George (1903 – 1950) was the pseudonym of Eric Blair. Educated at Eton, he joined the Burma Civil Police, an experience he used in his first novel *Burmese Days* (1934). His writings, beginning with *Down and Out in Paris and London* (1933) showed political commitment and a social concern for the realities of poverty, but, although he fought and was wounded in the Spanish Civil War (*Homage to Catalonia,* 1937), he was never a member of any political party. During the Second World War he worked as a journalist and broadcaster, becoming the finest political writer of his generation. He is world famous for his two, very different, novels about totalitarianism and its effects, *Animal Farm* (1945) and *Nineteen Eighty Four* (1949).

Owen Wilfred (1893 – 1918) was one of the generation of poets whose work, written in the trenches of the First World War, remains amongst the greatest war poetry ever written. He had early ambitions to be a poet, but the shock of the war produced a kind of writing that an upper-middle- class upbringing had not prepared him for. It is finely written, deeply compassionate, and ultimately modern in its vision of waste.

P _____

Poe Edgar Allan (1809 – 1849) is one of the best known of all American writers, but he achieved little success in his own lifetime, working for newspapers and magazines in various towns, and never enjoying any of the literary society of his home town of Boston. He published a great deal of work, largely short stories (detective tales, horror stories, and science fiction), a novel of the sea *The Narrative of Arthur Gordon Pym of Nantucket* (1838) and poetry. Despite his lack of initial success, Poe's work was astonishingly widespread in its influence, and many of his stories remain classics of their kind.

Pound Ezra (1885 – 1972) was born in Idaho, but grew up in Pennsylvania, where William Carlos Williams was one of his friends. He left America for Europe in 1908, and was not to return for 40 years. He became a leading figure in the Imagist movement, became well known in literary circles, and published a continual stream of volumes of verse. His work from this early period also includes translations and critical essays. Pound continued to write poetry, always experimenting with form and with subject matter, using a wide range of linguistic and literary influences for several decades. During the Second World War he became involved with the Axis forces, and after the war was confined in an asylum for several years, but he kept on writing until he completed his main work *The Cantos* in 1964.

R _____

Raine Craig was born in County Durham in 1944. He has published four volumes of poetry, which have established him as a witty and observant commentator on modern life.

Reid Alastair was born in Scotland in 1926. Among his volumes of verse are *Oddments, Inklings, Omens and Moments* and *Passwords.*

S _____

Sassoon Siegfried (1886 – 1967) is remembered for having encouraged Wilfred Owen in his writing, as well as for his own limited output of verse. Better known as a prose writer, his autobiographical volumes, often partly fictionalized, have continued to enjoy popularity, especially *The Memoirs of a Fox-Hunting Man* (1928) and *Sherston's Progress* (1936).

Shakespeare William (1564 – 1616) is the greatest name in English literature. He wrote some 37 plays (and collaborated on others), the best known sonnets in English, and some long poems. Born in Stratford-on-Avon, he retired there after his successful career in the theatre with the company known as the King's Men. His works were not written for publication, although many were printed during his lifetime. The First Folio of 1623 remains the principal source of most of Shakespeare's texts – it was prepared for publication by John Heminge and Henry Condell, to whom posterity owes an immeasurable debt. A great deal has been said about the disputed authorship of the works of Shakespeare – the fact that we know very little about the man and his life has given rise to a lot of speculation, most of it meaningless. 'The play's the thing', as Hamlet says – and Shakespeare's plays are the greatest the world has known. Here is a list of some of the best known. Comedies: *A Midsummer Night's Dream, The Merchant of Venice, As You Like It, Twelfth Night, The Merry Wives of Windsor, The Taming of the Shrew, Measure for Measure, The Winter's Tale, The Tempest.* Tragedies: *Romeo and Juliet, Hamlet, Othello, King Lear, Macbeth.* Roman Plays: *Julius Caesar, Antony and Cleopatra, Coriolanus.* Histories: *Richard III, Richard II, Henry IV, Henry V.*

Smith Stevie (1902 – 1971) was an unusual figure, a poet whose simplicity is belied by the occasional poem of great resonance; an unmarried woman who lived with an aunt in North London, she seems to resemble Emily Dickinson, but wrote much less than the American poet. She also wrote some remarkable novels, the best of which is *Novel on Yellow Paper* (1936), which, like her best poetry, is shot through with a kind of sad gaiety, an enigmatic humour, and a kind of deliberate carelessness.

Spark Muriel was born in Edinburgh in 1918, and began her literary career after the Second World War, writing literary biography before moving on to the novel and short story forms in which she made her name. Her works tend to examine the pressure on characters of time, or of a forceful personality, as is the case in *The Prime of Miss Jean Brodie* (1962), which was also a successful play, film and television series. Among her best known novels are *Memento Mori, The Girls of Slender Means* and *The Mandelbaum Gate.*

Steinbeck John (1902 – 1968) was a Californian, and many of his novels and stories are set among the poorer people of that state. His tales, such as *Cannery Row* (1944) and *Of Mice and Men* (1937) show a great, almost Dickensian, sympathy for the downtrodden and underprivileged, which found its greatest expression in the epic novel of agricultural unemployment and migration, *The Grapes of Wrath* (1939), one of the best American novels of the twentieth century. Steinbeck won the Nobel Prize for Literature in 1962.

Stevenson Robert Louis (1850 – 1894) was born in Edinburgh, married in California, and died in the South Sea island of Samoa. He is remembered for some marvellous adventure stories such as *Kidnapped* (1886) and *Treasure Island* (1883) as well as for the travel books *Travels with a Donkey in the Cevennes* (1879), the short novel *Dr Jekyll and Mr Hyde* (1886), the classic *The Amateur Emigrant* (1892), and the unfinished novel of Calvinism and guilt, *Weir of Hermiston*, published in 1896.

W

Waugh Evelyn (1903 – 1966) wrote some of the liveliest comic novels of the 1930s, brilliantly satirizing the upper-class society of the day. His best-known work, *Brideshead Revisited* (1945) reflects his interest in Catholic themes, and shows the serious intent that lay behind his comedy. Other well-known titles include *Decline and Fall* (1928), *The Loved One* (1948), and *Unconditional Surrender* (1961).

Wilde Oscar (1854 – 1900) was born in Ireland and made his name as a leader of the Aesthetic movement in London after leaving Oxford University in 1878. He worked as editor of a women's magazine for some time, but gained his literary reputation with the publication of his famous short stories, of which *The Canterville Ghost* (1887) and *The Happy Prince* (1888) are the best known, with his novel *The Picture of Dorian Gray* (1891), and above all, with the great comedies which brought his famous epigrammatic wit to a wide audience: *Lady Windermere's Fan* (1892), *A Woman of No Importance* (1893), *An Ideal Husband* (1895), and *The Importance of Being Earnest* (1895). Wilde was convicted of homosexual offences in 1895 and spent two years in prison. *The Ballad of Reading Gaol* (1898) and the long letter, more an essay, known as *De Profundis* (published incomplete in 1905, complete only in 1962) date from this period. Wilde died in Paris after spending the last three years of his life wandering around Europe.

Williams William Carlos (1883 – 1963) was the son of an Englishman who lived in the USA, and was educated in Europe and America, following a career in medicine in New Jersey for many years. His writings, in poetry and the novel, are ambitiously experimental, often expressionistic and minimalist in appearance, but bringing into play a wealth of connotations and unexpected associations. He is best remembered as a poet, but his novels, although never achieving the recognition accorded to the poetry, are a significant contribution to the development of the psychologically realistic genre.

Woolf (Adeline) Virginia (1882 – 1941) was born at Hyde Park Gate, London. At the age of 13 she suffered a breakdown following her mother's death. She had been very close to her mother, who had kept the household in order to relieve all possible strain on her father who was labouring all hours of the day on *The Dictionary of National Biography*. Julia Stephen's death threw the house into disorder and Virginia's breakdown was the result. The shadow of instability came like a cloud at different stages of her career. Sir Leslie Stephen died in 1904 and the shadow appeared again, but in December of that year her first published work, an unsigned review, appeared in the *Manchester Guardian*. Virginia's career as a writer continued with *Night and Day* (1919), the stories collected in *Monday or Tuesday* (1921), *Jacob's Room* (1922), *Mrs Dalloway* (1925), and *To the Lighthouse* (1927). *Orlando* (1928) is unlike any other novels and was her greatest commercial success. The full title is *Orlando: A Biography*, and the book is dedicated to the author's lover, Vita Sackville-West. It is in some senses an extended love letter, with the great house of the novel identifiable as Knole, the ancestral home of the Sackvilles in Kent. *Flush: A Biography* (1933) is the 'biography' of Elizabeth Barrett Browning's spaniel, and gives a dog's-eye view of the love affair of his mistress and Robert Browning. It is a warm and gentle book and, like *Orlando*, another expression of Virginia Woolf's manifold talents.

Wordsworth William (1770 – 1850), the greatest of the Romantic poets, was born in Cockermouth, Cumberland, in the area of the Lake District, with which his name was to become very strongly associated. Indeed, most of his life was spent in the Lake District, apart from his many trips to France (1791–92) and Germany (1798–99); (the dates are of the earliest and most influential trips). He made his home with his sister Dorothy at Grasmere, and the area became a place of literary pilgrimage, much celebrated in Wordsworth's own works as well as those of many other writers. Wordsworth continued to write poetry all through his long life, constantly adding to the long autobiographical poem *The Prelude*: largely written between 1799 and 1805, it was not published until just after his death. With the poems in the epoch-making volume *Lyrical Ballads* (with Coleridge, 1798), this is his major contribution to English literature. But his output was vast, and several of his longer poems, such as *Michael*, a pastoral poem (1800), and *The Excursion* (1814) are of considerable importance. He also wrote critical essays, and journals of his later travels in Europe; but in old age his capacities declined, and his later works do not reach the very high levels of inspiration and achievement of his earlier poetry.

Y

Yeats W(illiam) B(utler) (1865 – 1939) was one of the great literary figures of his age, and was closely involved with the political and cultural life of his native Ireland during the time of its struggle for independence. He had been an associate of the Aesthetes in the 1890s, was closely connected with attempts to revive Irish drama in the early years of the twentieth century, and late in life became a Senator of the Republic of Ireland. His continual output of poetry was central to all these aspects of his busy career – of his many volumes *The Wild Swans at Coole* (1917 – 19), *Michael Robartes and the Dancer* (1921) and *The Tower* (1928) contain his best work.

Throughout these notes line references to texts in the book are shown in brackets.

CHAPTER 1 SENSE AND NONSENSE

1

Students should not open their books until 1.6.

The first text should be presented preferably on the blackboard/whiteboard or OHP as a straightforward note, so that students are not influenced by seeing it as a poem: the 'note' must be taken as simply as possible, just as a message, which might have been left on a kitchen table.

1.1

Open response. It is interesting how much answers can vary, and the attitudes these answers reveal: husband to wife (or at any rate, man to woman) predominates, rather than, for example, child to parent. It can be stimulating to examine why the intuitions are as they are.

The message, in functional terms, is an apology, although, as we shall see, it goes a fair way beyond that basic communicative function.

1.2

The shortest possible version might be, 'Sorry, I ate the plums' (although many of us would not have said anything at all!). This leaves out the understanding of what the plums were for, where they were (*icebox* is American English; in British English 'fridge' or 'refrigerator' would be used), the strong *Forgive me*, and the final rather sensual words.

The word *just* can, of course, be omitted. Some students bring up the fact that it already contains something apologetic in itself, but we do not want to go too deeply into single words just yet!

1.3

Still without looking at the text as a poem, students can experiment with word-grouping, lines, and even word order if they wish (some re-ordering can be allowed – but keep it to a minimum).

1.4

What will emerge is how the impact of the words can be influenced by layout, punctuation, length of line, and so on. Some students will prefer the message as it was – just as a note. This is fine, if they can suggest or explain why.

1.5

They give a new, unexpected tone of sensuality – of the pleasure of eating the plums. In general, they are understood as positive, the word *cold* being the most surprising, and the most positive.

Do not encourage symbolic readings and speculations at this stage!

1.6

Students open their books at this point.
Open response, deriving from reflection so far.

1.7

It is *This Is Just to Say* – the capital letters and line spacing are all that distinguish it from a line in the poem. Students may be encouraged to suggest possible titles: *The Plums in the Icebox*, and the like, might emerge.

1.8

There is remarkably little punctuation in Williams' versions. Only the capital F (9) indicates a new 'sentence'. The note version given earlier was punctuated according to 'normal' rules. Ask students to express a preference, with reasons.

1.9

In that William Carlos Williams published it as a poem, it is a poem. Students might be surprised to learn that it was written in the 1920s. The point is to notice how a simple message can become a poem, and vice versa. Students' preconceived ideas about 'poetry' should be a little shaken by this – and poetry might be a little demystified for them. This should continue with the next texts.

Writing poetry as if it were not poetry is a teaching/study technique which can be used with many texts. We have not employed it directly with other texts in this book, but individual teachers (and students) might like to bear it in mind for future reference.

2

As these poems are largely visual they have not been recorded. Edwin Morgan calls them poems; reasons should be given why students agree or disagree.

2.1

Open response, students picking out what strikes them most. It is important not to worry about unknown vocabulary.

2.2

Open response. Stress that 'meaning' and 'seriousness' are not always vitally important! *Spacepoem 3: Off Course* is usually seen as more serious, however.

2.3

A storyline might be that a spacecraft and crew hit some unexplained trouble which sends them into the wrong orbit. Their destiny is left open. (The typographical layout also moves 'off course' in the last lines.) The article/adjective/noun pattern in itself is interesting. There are no verbs. Adjectival forms of verbs can be found, e.g. *crackling, turning. Mouth-organ, beard, pitch, song* are among repeated words. The collocations are sometimes varied, showing the movement of the narration from normal to off course.

Off course sounds similar to 'of course': the pun is on normality and divergence.

2.4

Open response. The titles actually **give** meaning to the texts.

2.5

Open response. Possible ideas: butterflies, breakfast, flower, steps, woman, windsurf, etc.

3 🖭

The unexpected nature of the text means that pre-reading stimuli are superfluous. After students have listened to the poem once, elicit immediate reactions without reference to the written text.

Ideas such as trains, meaningless nonsense, lunatic communication, might come out. Have students keep note of all responses for later reference.

3.1

Open response. Point out how naturally the reader **tries** to give/find meaning: discuss if texts (paintings, etc.) have to have meaning. This could get too wide-ranging and abstract, but can be useful in making students think about the nature of meaning.

3.2

Open response. The result is probably a mixture of curiosity and frustration. Do not dwell on it too long, but these impressions will be useful!

3.3

This encourages students to be rather more specific about the meaning of the text and to think directly about the connection between the title and text. Discuss the implication of the title, both before and after examining vocabulary. A pavan is a kind of stately dance, or the music for it: there is a clear reference to a piece of music by Maurice Ravel, *Pavan for a Dead Infanta* (1899). This could provoke discussion on a more concentrated level about possible meanings of the poem. (Prompts: the contrast between dead/unborn; who is speaking? why a dance? why sometimes Chi-chi and An-an and sometimes Chi-an? etc.) The results will probably stress mother-child relationships, among other themes. If this is clearly a result, underline the tendency to relate meaning to human experience. Why should we concentrate on *human* experience? Does a male-female relationship emerge?

3.4

Chi-chi and An-an were two giant pandas, she (Chi-chi) belonging to London Zoo, he to Moscow Zoo. Attempts to mate them at London Zoo were widely publicized in the early 1970s, but were unsuccessful. Hence the *unborn* infanta.

Have students trace their story through the poem. Is the title appropriate?

3.5

Elicit whether the 'key' to the poem reduces its meaning potential or provides clarification. Explore the meaning, expanding on themes which now emerge: courtship, loneliness, unsatisfactory relationships, sexuality, even East-West *détente/entente!* Elicit whether (and, if so, how and why) students identify with anything in the poem. The themes listed above can be useful prompts.

3.6

Open response. Discussion might arise on deliberate hiding of meaning – MacBeth usually explains the key to the poem before reading it, so the obfuscation is not his! Is it essential that meaning always be clear and simple? Students' awareness by now should lead them to reject that idea.

3.7

Open response. Was it a waste of time, or an enjoyable exercise?

4 🖭

A mouse's tail.

4.1

Rewrite showing the rhymes.
It is sad perhaps because it ends with a threat of death.

4.2

Open response.

4.3 🖭

Students will sympathize largely with Alice, as she seems to be a kind of victim of the Hare's and the Hatter's sententiousness.

4.4

This opens up the fascinating question of what is the meaning of meaning. It should not be examined too deeply: students should be made aware of the openness and flexibility of meaning and of its frequent elusiveness. There are no fixed meanings: everyone in the class has a different idea of 'cat', for instance, which goes far beyond its dictionary definition or denotation.

4.5

No, it is never answered.
a She is at first keen to answer it, then led astray.
b Open response, generally a bit frustrated!

4.6

Open response. The likeliest answer is 'I don't think I ever have . . .'.

4.7

Nonsense implies the absence of normal codes of language, behaviour, etc.
Alice is a rather typical well-brought-up child of the Victorian period, intimidated by the Hare and Hatter, and shocked by the potential anarchy of the question *"Why not?"* and by the upsetting of normality it involves. This might be suggested as a reason for her silence.

5 🖭

5.1

a There was a young lady whose chin
    Resembled the point of a pin;
    So she had it made sharp, and purchased a harp,
    And played several tunes with her chin.

b There was an old man in a boat,
Who said, 'I'm afloat, I'm afloat!'
When they said, 'No, you ain't,' he was ready to faint,
That unhappy old man in a boat.

5.2

First words: There was . . .
Number of lines: 4
Rhythm: da DA da da DA da da DA
         da DA da da DA da da DA
         da DA da da DA
         da DA da da DA
         da DA da da DA da da DA
Rhyme: a - a - b - b - a
Standard ingredients of limericks are:
a the main character, introduced as a young/old person, man or lady;
b the second line usually providing information about him or her, often in the form of a relative clause;
c the third line normally coinciding with the climax, the memorable action or phrase (either the character does something, or people are brought in with their comments, questions, doubts);
d the adjective in line 4, with its incongruous quality on which much of the enjoyment of the reader, and presumably of the author, depends.

If certain 'musts' are observed in standard wording and patterning – the rhyme, the beats, the dancing rhythm of line 3 – and some freedom is allowed in lines 2 and 4, it should not be difficult to try one's hand at limericks.

5.3

Open response.

CHAPTER 2 PLEASURES

1 🖸

1.1

The answer is in the second-last line of the poem:
a poor life.
Elicit whether students agree or disagree, and reasons.

1.2

This calls for an imaginative rather than a literal response. A student might say that the poet sees the sky reflected or the water twinkling in the sunlight – the play of light on water – the streams are not literally full of stars! This is the first example of figurative use of language students have found, so its effects should be emphasized and illustrated, perhaps with students' examples from their own language.

1.3

Capitalization gives the idea of Beauty as a general concept rather than a specific example of beauty. Notice it is feminine (*her*, 10, 11 and 12). This is an example of personification.

1.4

Open response. Possible expressions: 'hang around', 'laze', 'think about nothing', 'daydream', etc.

1.5

Open response. Looking around, enjoying your surroundings, relaxing.

2 🖸

Because people are as vulnerable as flies.

2.1

Only b*rush'd*, *Shall* and *Am not I...?* are a little unusual. Their modern equivalents would be: brushed; Till some blind hand brushes my wing; Aren't I...? Archaic uses of 'thee'/'thou' will be found frequently in texts in this book.

2.2

a Little fly, my thoughtless hand has brushed away your summer's play.
b Since/Because (9); lack/absence (15)
c If we assume that . . . (13); whether (19, 20)
Lines 11 and 12 would read 'Till some blind hand brushes my wing.' *Then am I* (17) would read 'Then I am.'

2.3

a It was brushed away by the poet's hand.
b The poet.
c No.
d They are equally vulnerable, at the mercy of chance incidents.
e Freedom and happiness, music and enjoyment.
f Both poems celebrate the positive side of life. They are similar in their affirmation of happiness. Lines 13 – 20 introduce a note of ambiguity or doubt (signalled by *if*, 13). Students might want to explore this more deeply, or might prefer to leave it alone.

2.4

It is unspecified, the *hand* being a metaphor for any kind of mischance or accident (or death) that may happen. (In the abstract, it might be generalized as 'destiny'.)
Thoughtless seems to refer specifically to the action of brushing away the fly – an action that the speaker is unconscious of performing. Whereas *want of thought*, meaning the **lack** or **absence** of thought, suggests human consciousness as a more general concept.
Discussion should focus on elements of symmetry and contrast in the poem. Bring out such things as fly/man; summer's play/thoughtless hand; dancing, drinking, singing/dying; thinking/not thinking.
The richness of the poem lies in the fact that although it seems simple superficially, more complex meaning is suggested through its ambiguity.

2.5

The first one is the closest definition, but all four statements have some validity.
Yes, the poet probably is happy. Discussion on the quality of happiness. It is important to see that the poems **seem**

simple but deal with profound themes which go beyond the simple words.

2.6

This is intended as experiment, stimulus, and discussion. Students compare their own versions of *The Fly* and *Leisure* with the originals and with their colleagues' versions.

3 📼

The Owl and the Pussycat is of course 'nonsense', but students will be able to trace the through-line of a love story: elopement, proposal, and marriage. Bring out romantic elements – singing to a guitar, dancing hand-in-hand, etc. – and elicit their effect in relation to the characters enacting them, i.e. how it makes them seem human. Can one of the two be identified as male, the other as female? If so, how? Discuss whether the answers so far are influenced by preconceptions and expectations, i.e. by echoes in the students' minds from previous reading, or cultural background. Is it a children's poem?

3.1

They sail for 17 lines, *a year and a day* (16), until they reach *the land where the Bong-tree grows* (17), where the rest of the story is set. The only localities visited in the land of the Bong-tree are the wood, possibly the hill (although the Turkey might have performed marriage ceremonies away from home), and the sand, presumably near where they left their pea-green boat.

3.2

Four: owl, pussycat, pig, turkey.
The pig appears to stand in a wood with a ring at the end of his nose. However, he enjoys the exercise of free will and is at complete liberty to sell his ring.
The turkey performs marriage ceremonies, which might or might not indicate something about his role in society. See if students find it amusing (or just silly) to try to 'read in' social roles for the characters.

3.3

The characters and their roles, the invented words and place names. The nonsense is somehow acceptable as such, without a search for deeper meaning. What allows the reader to accept it just as simple nonsense (for example, rhyme, rhythm, etc.)?

3.4

Vocabulary:
fowl = bird
tarried = delayed/waited/put off
mince = shredded meat
quince = a kind of fruit
runcible = no synonym exists, as *runcible* is an invented word (entertainingly, the *Oxford English Dictionary* gives a definition – 'fork curved like a spoon, with three broad prongs, one edged' – but with no clear etymology).
Do any other words seem to be inventions, e.g. *Bong-tree*, *Piggy-wig*? Why do students think Lear invents words? The question of rhythm might be raised again here: a

three-syllable adjective is necessary for the rhythm of line 28. Students could try inventing others, and see if any sound better than *runcible*. However, they must be long - short - short, dactylic in stress.

3.5

Apart from obvious references to singing and dancing, the rhymes, rhythm, repetitions, and refrains might be mentioned. Students might like to mark the beats or stresses of the rhythm throughout (long, short) to bring out the musical regularity Lear gives the verses. (Following the text while listening will be helpful here.)

3.6

Students' production, leading to comparison with the original.

4

This passage is rather more philosophical in content, containing something of an 'aesthetic' message – but this need not be gone into too deeply.
Dorian should: look after his beauty; *realize* his youth (36); and 'live' (1 to the end).
He should not: get sunburnt (1) or *squander* his youth (36 – 37 ff.).

4.1

When he loses his youth and his beauty, according to Lord Henry, he will also lose his happiness (see 28 – 32).

4.2

Open response. This kind of idealism usually finds an echo in younger readers' minds!

4.3

Some day (10) is contrasted with *now* (13); the present is positive, the future negative. This is the fundamental time content of the whole passage, and is also brought out in the tenses of the verbs used. *A few years* (27) is all the time Dorian will have – *every month* (32) lessening his beauty and, thereby, his happiness. *Time is jealous of you* (33) could be seen as the climax of this discussion on time.

4.4

It would, in Lord Henry's view, be *unbecoming* (2).
Open response. Attractiveness is a culturally conditioned idea, and discussion of various cultures' notions of beauty can be developed, models evaluated, and differences compared.

4.5

Open response.
. . . when thought has seared your forehead (11)
Beauty is a form of Genius (15)
. . . that silver shell we call the moon (18)
contain some exaggeration in their rhetoric which may be contrasted with, for example, the directness of the last three lines.

4.6

Open response. Lord Henry is older than Dorian, as might be deduced from his attitude to the loss of youth.

4.7

Oscar Wilde's aphorisms can be seen as controversial, witty, or banal. *It is only shallow people who do not judge by appearances* (24) is one of his most famous paradoxes. All these sentences balance beauty/youth and time/loss in an argument in favour of youth and of living for the moment. (This could usefully be cross-referenced with some of the texts, and the discussion, in Chapter 8.)

4.8

The happiness of youth and thoughtless freedom. Discussion could focus on the transience of such happiness and/or the necessity of enjoying each moment as it comes. Elicit whether students feel the passage as a whole is positive or negative. Usually the reaction is positive, but with some acknowledgement of the regret at the passing of time contained in Lord Henry's words.

5 📼

Notice Millamant is the woman, Mirabell the man. The list Millamant makes could be summed up more or less as follows: getting up when she wants; no endearments; no public displays of affection; no visits (to other people, the theatre, etc.) together; freedom to see and write to anyone; to dress as she likes; to have her own friends (not his); to eat when she likes; and to have her own privacy. Most students (especially female students) will find the list intelligent and right.

5.1

Open response. Generally positive, although weaker than Millamant.

5.2

Open response.

5.3

Open response. Millamant is rather forthright and therefore not very traditional. Indeed it is the traditional aspects of married life that she wants to avoid.

5.4

It is not necessary to go into any historical depth or detail here, impressions are all that is required. The society is upper-class, with an emphasis on socializing – seeing and being seen, appearances being important. So, superficial, artificial, old-fashioned, insincere, might be offered as judgements on it.
Open response. It is comic with a serious intent. Congreve uses the speech to parody this kind of society.

5.5

In order:

thee	fond	wits
bid you . . . adieu	folks	closet
indolent slumbers	well-bred	sole empress
a-bed	hitherto	leave
as	trifles	articles subscribed
nauseous cant	interrogatories	dwindle
fulsomely	wry faces	

CHAPTER 3 EDUCATION

1 📼

It is interesting to bring out the contrast between the learning process (learning to play) and the pleasure of playing. This is to some extent analogous with students' literary development.

1.1

Give more regard to movement
Forget and let the sound flow
Let go
Be silent
Feel what is happening

1.2

Open response. Expansion and discussion.
This discussion should help to make students aware of the difference between **feeling** as a reaction to a poem and thinking, or studying, too closely. These questions are designed to elicit the effect of the poem on the reader without his/her necessarily understanding every word or every idea contained in it. See Introduction on Vocabulary p. *vi*.

1.3

It is not easy to make specific changes. To a certain extent Reid wants the description of the playing and the child's reaction to it to have a similar effect to the effect of the music. As the poem progresses, the reader/listener is more and more involved with the hypothetical music, and his/her reactions are led by the poet's instructions: the reader becomes more and more the addressee of the poem – the child at the piano.

1.4

Time has the usual sense in *this time* (1) and a musical sense in line 3. The other phrases have an effectiveness as they stand, which is difficult to render through synonyms, paraphrases, or translations. In 19, *glooms* makes a verb out of a noun.
Particular uses of words might be examined, but this is as good a point as any to have students realize that it is not essential to look up every unknown word, to translate unusual phrases (3 – 4, for instance), or to rearrange poetic word order (*letting flow the sound*, 6 – 7) in order to get something out of the text. Lines 10 – 12 give the only proper similes.

1.5

Open response, but the end of each verse requires a silence. Discuss and evaluate other suggestions.

1.6

Open response.

2 📼

Miss Mackay (pronounced Mk'ai) is the headmistress. Most students will have mixed reactions to Miss Brodie: she is untraditional, independent, and strong-minded, but this might not be to everyone's taste!

2.1

To *the group* in the next sentence.

2.2

The reference is to the custom of walking in file with two or three students side by side.
She is therefore leading a group of her pupils and talking to two of these schoolgirls, named Sandy and Rose.

2.3

It seems to be a difficult relationship between superior (Miss Mackay) and subordinate (Miss Brodie), with essential differences of opinion. Miss Brodie's attitude should emerge as fairly complacent, self-satisfied, detached, but aggressive. The words *summoned* and *morning break* (4), with their bureaucratic overtones, signal the superior/inferior role and the setting.

2.4

It is a kind of reversal of what has been said, in that Miss Brodie obviously intends her hearers to accept **her** view of education rather than Miss Mackay's. So the author shows that Miss Brodie **does** put ideas into her girls' heads. The tone is slightly ironic.

2.5

The expression 'put ideas into someone's head' generally has a negative connotation. By using it Miss Mackay is expressing her disapproval of Miss Brodie's method.

2.6

Complacent, sure of herself, aggressive. Discussion might focus on how much a teacher can/should impose her/his own ideas, and how much influence such ideas can have on students. She implies that she does not want to thrust her own ideas on her pupils: she wants them to think for themselves, to encourage independent thinking.

2.7

Open response. It is interesting to see how old students think Miss Brodie is; she is, in fact, in her mid-thirties.

3 💻

The pupils are boisterous rather than intimidated – indeed, it is they who try to intimidate the new teacher.

3.1

All points of view might be substantiated, **d** perhaps the least convincingly. (NB Half a crown was the equivalent of 12½ pence.)

3.2

Part of the truth: he has found the secret of managing them, although finding it was not exactly easy.

3.3

They probably fear him. At least they know they cannot get the better of him.

3.4

Where Grimes calls them a *little mob* (1), talks of letting them out (as if they were animals), and abjures teaching, Mr Prendergast's attitude seems less extreme: he calls them *those boys* (74) and appreciates Paul's potential difficulties, but nothing stronger than that. Paul's attitude changes within the passage from terrified (9 – 10) to amiable (14) to irritable (18 and 25 – 30) to desperate (45) to angry (59) to despondent (69) to apparently unconcerned (76).

3.5

Open response. Compare the kinds of 'education' read about so far. Where would least be learnt? (Probably here.)

3.6

See Introduction on Vocabulary p. *vi*.

4 💻

Nicholas clearly does not want to show his feelings too much, but we feel he reacts negatively – as we do – to Squeers.

4.1

Open response. Reactions will be largely of amusement.

4.2

Lines 22 – 32 in particular; lines 42 – 56 highlight the false side of this system. Mr Squeers' *long pause* (61) might indicate that he is aware of the system's defects, but is going to continue in his own way nevertheless.

4.3

Both are intended only to keep the pupils occupied, rather than to teach them.
Squeers exploits his pupils. In the Waugh passage, the pupils and masters balance each other out in terms of authority and threats.

4.4

Open response. This is a kind of summary, of character, rather than of story. Adjectives which might help (but not necessarily for **both** characters!): authoritarian, self-righteous, proud, stupid, intelligent, sensitive, insensitive, caring, interested, self-centred, open, narrow-minded, modern, old-fashioned.

4.5

Open response. More pity for the pupils is evoked here, because Nicholas pities the boys, whereas Paul sees them as a challenge, and we judge them more at a distance. The first person narration gives the reader a closer understanding of, and therefore sympathy with, the boys.

4.6

This is a common technique in Dickens; it shows a kind of distance between simple reality, e.g. words like *showed* and *movement*, and the heightened effect of the more unusual words *evinced* and *locomotion*. It is this distance which gives the scene its comic potential. Other examples of unusual words might include *commodity* (12), *scour* (30), *casement* (31), *quadruped* (47).

Examples where two words are placed together might be *locomotion or playfulness* (6), *their places and their books* (11), *half cunning and half doubtful* (58 – 59). Their effect can be one of emphasis, repeating the same idea, or of adding another aspect to the first part of the expression. They are an economical descriptive technique, working by association and contrast.

5 ▣

The voice is the teacher's, and *they* are the pupils.

5.1

They are compared to hunting dogs: *my pack of unruly hounds* (3).
The hunting dog imagery explores the semantic field of pulling and pushing, impatience and reluctance which indicates the pupils' unwillingness.
Possible clues that students might pick out are: *hounds* (3), *hunt* (4), *tugged* (2), *quarry* (4), *strained* (2), *pack* (3), *unruly* (3).

5.2

Open response.

5.3

Care (see line 24).

5.4

Open response.

5.5

Opinions can differ here: some will say that it denies the speaker's earlier wish to escape, turning to resignation and waiting; others will suggest that it confirms what has been said, reinforcing the ideas of resignation, lack of interest, and indifference. Discussion may be focused on indifference as a strong/weak emotion. Have students ever imagined what teachers feel – about teaching **and** about them?

CHAPTER 4 PERSPECTIVES

1 ▣

Recall of the Blake poem read in Chapter 2 will be useful. Reading by separate groups can lead to comparison of titles, subject matter, and the effect of each poem.
The basic difference is that the first poem is happy, while the second is sad.

1.1

Open response.

1.2

thee = you (see Chapter 2, 2)
befall = happen to
but = only
dost = do (*thou dost smile* = you smile)
the while = at the same time
Infant Sorrow is poetic in its uses (*piping loud* instead of 'loudly'), but contains no actual archaic forms apart from the elision in *groan'd* (1).

1.3

Infant Joy has two speakers, the two-day-old child (1 – 2, 4 – 5) and the *I* of the second verse. Both speak in the present tense, in a positive way. Both voices in *Infant Joy* 'sing', in so much as they both celebrate the happy birth, life, and joy of the infant.
Infant Sorrow has one speaker, the *I*, who speaks in the past tense. The title leads us to expect that this 'voice' is still an infant, but the speaker might be an adult recounting past experience, negative throughout.

1.4

Dictionary work. Negative words:
groan'd (1)
wept (1)
dangerous (2*)*
helpless (3)
piping (3) – the sense here is 'crying'
fiend (4)
hid (4)
struggling (5)
striving (6)
swadling (6) = tight wrapping, restricting baby's movement (the usual spelling is 'swaddling')
bound (7) – continuing the restrictive idea of 'swadling bands'
weary (7)
sulk (8)

1.5

Summary.
Sweet joy befall thee means 'may good and happy things happen to you'. This projects into the future the ideas expressed in the earlier lines. *Like a fiend hid in a cloud* means 'like a little devil hidden in the air', which gives a **visual** image of the infant born in the preceding lines. *To sulk upon my mother's breast* gives the idea of the **opposite** of normal behaviour: instead of taking positive nourishment from his (or her – the gender is not given)

mother's breast, this infant has an attitude of rejection and complaint.

1.6

Open response, but clearly neither is a 'true' representation, if only because the fact of the infants' speaking is unrealistic. The attitudes, however, can be discussed in realistic terms, especially in relation to future experience. (These texts can usefully be related to Chapter 7, 5 either now or later).

2 🖥️

There are some American English usages and dialect forms here: *don't* for 'doesn't'; *she give it right to me* for 'she gave it to me'; *nuts* for 'mad'; *cause* for 'because'. Steinbeck is describing helplessness, creating sympathy for an outsider, one who can never participate in the normal world, but who is actually a deeply caring and sensitive being. Yet Lennie is obviously dangerous – this is the paradox on which the story turns.

2.1

Initially she thinks he is a little mad (*nuts*, 2), and so is afraid of him, although she likes him (*you're a kinda nice fella*, 14). This underlines the basic contrast between Lennie's simplicity and the element of risk.

2.2

Possible moments include *Lennie chuckled with pleasure* (8), when he remembers the velvet.
This changes when he recalls, *I lost it* (12). Similarly, when stroking Curley's wife's hair (23 ff.), he is happy until she reacts to his hanging on (29), which leads to his panic (31).

2.3

Open response. Probably he is afraid of being punished, especially when he says, *I done* [= I did] *another bad thing* (53). *Another* implies something like this has happened before.

2.4

No.
He just does not know his own strength, and gets carried away, losing control when she reacts against his stroking her hair too heavily. He wants to stroke velvet and to *tend . . . rabbits* (39), but his gentleness suddenly, as here, becomes unwittingly violent. He gets angry (41, 44*)* because he cannot control the object of his affections or his own strength.

2.5

Summary. This can be as short as two or three sentences.

2.6

Open response and discussion. Lennie's innocence should be brought out, as well as the contrast between pity and terror which he evokes.

3

The secret is revealed by the cat hidden behind the wall. The story can be approached in different ways: reading then working through the questions, or (and this will create more suspense) reading and answering 3.1 paragraph by paragraph.

3.1

1st paragraph
She is his wife. The cat almost trips him up, making him nearly fall *down the steep stairs* to the cellar. He kills his wife because of his anger at her interference, which prevents him killing the cat (so the wife substitutes the cat as the killer's victim!).

2nd paragraph
Removing it from the house; burning it in small pieces; burying it in the cellar; throwing it into the well; sending it away in a box; finally, the method he decides on is hiding it behind a new purpose-built wall in the cellar.

3rd and 4th paragraphs
Yes, because of the new plaster, and the projection which had been filled up: he just has to remove then replace these bricks.

5th and 6th paragraphs
To kill it. He feels greatly relieved, free and happy that he cannot find it.

7th and 8th paragraphs
By behaving calmly, impassively, and even striking the wall behind which the body was hidden.

9th and 10th paragraphs
His striking the wall made the cat, which had been walled up with the wife's body, cry out, revealing the hiding-place to the police, who found the body, and the cat, which, of course, was still alive.

3.2

Open response and discussion.
Key words/ideas might be:
a arrogant, over-confident
b instrument of vengeance, evil spirit, symbol of conscience
c chilling, an examination of guilt, eerie

3.3

Open response. Reactions are usually ambiguous, and this was probably Poe's intention. Many readers sympathize with the cat – is this just an animal-lover's reaction?

3.4

Both the cat and guilt/self-punishment can be justified, as can *a reward for his arrogance*.
Open response and discussion, leading to summary.

4 📼

The 'game' of recognition which Raine's Martian creates
would be destroyed if it were explained word by word. But
the first six lines describe books and their effects,
including tears and laughter; there follow descriptions of
mist and rain, a car, a watch, a telephone, the toilet (seen
by the Martian as suffering), sleep, and dreams.

4.1 _____

Lines 1 – 6 describe books, some (2) with pictures
(*markings*) which give them greater value, and some which
make people cry (3) and laugh (4).
Lines 13 – 16 describe a car, its *key* (to make it start) and
its speed of movement.

4.2 _____

Open response. See lines 11 – 12 and 17 – 18.

4.3 _____

Open response. See lines 25 – 30 (toilet) and 31 – 34
(sleeping and dreaming).

4.4 _____

The telephone.

4.5 _____

Open response and discussion.

4.6 _____

Open response.
Anything could be handled like this: aeroplanes, babies,
computers, etc. Suggest experimentation with: a football
match/a disco/a classroom/a traffic jam/a party.

4.7 _____

Open response. Notice that the line generally breaks with a
verb or a verb phrase, and that the next line begins with an
adverb or adverbial phrase.

5 _____

The story recalls the proverb 'the other man's grass is
always greener'. It goes straight to the heart of the matter:
the quest for the mysterious *spot of radiance*. The search is
brief; the discovery human, real, and both disappointing
and surprising.
The piazza is the verandah or balcony of the narrator's
house.

5.1 _____

Probably just the way the light and shade focused on the
spot, which turned out to be Marianna's window.

5.2 _____

The narrator's house, which seemed like *King Charming's
palace* (70).

5.3 _____

The sea: lines 23, 26, and 31
Travelling (apart from by sea): lines 33 – 36
Mythology: lines 12, 15 – 18, 23 – 24, 27 – 29, 37 – 39,
46 – 48
They add an idea of discovery, of magic and strangeness,

in contrast with the two very ordinary houses (the
narrator's and Marianna's) which are the actual setting of
the story.

5.4 _____

The vocabulary in this exercise is fairly difficult, so
teachers may want to anticipate all of it, or some of it,
before reading the text.
snugged = treasured
hopper-like hollow = low-lying area shaped like a round tube
mole = small dark mark
wan = pale, tired-looking
launch my yawl = set sail in my small boat
ho, cheerly, heart! = come on! (to a sailing crew)
sallying = going out
brakes = hedges and bushes
dwell = live
palanquin = small box for one person to be carried in
gilds = makes golden
as you will = whatever you wish

5.5 _____

These, like the elements in 5.3 give a wider frame of
reference to the mundane level of the story's setting. The
Potosi mine in Bolivia was the richest silver mine in the
world. In 1600 Potosi was the second largest city in the
world.
Edmund Spenser was an English poet (*c.*1552 – 1599) who
wrote *The Faerie Queen* (1590 – 1596). Both references are
historically distant (and to almost exactly the same 'golden
age'), as well as indicating another kind of world.
Similarly Una (37) is a reference to *The Faerie Queen*,
Book 1, where she represents true religion, purity and
faith, who is first separated from then reunited with the
Redcrosse Knight of Holiness. Perhaps in making this
reference the narrator wishes to identify himself with the
chivalrous and holy knight in the fable.
King Charming (70) (often merely Prince Charming)
recalls the story of Cinderella, where he rescues the
heroine from a miserable poor existence.
Open response leading to 5.6.

5.6 _____

These expressions confirm the fable/magic context of the
reference annotated in 5.5. Similar expressions can be
found in lines 46 – 47, 70, and elsewhere. These are mixed
with the through-line of the story to give the balance of
effects: there is a straightforward storyline from the time
references at the beginning to the anticlimax of lines 37 –
48, through to the final phrase *as you will* (87), which
balances the dilemma between *strange fancies* and *strange
things*.

5.7 _____

The previous answer might suggest an approach to the
summary – does leaving out the 'fancy' elements and
references limit the story too much?
Discussion and evaluation.

5.8

Open response. All the texts in this chapter could be read symbolically to some extent.
Do students like to do this, or do they react against symbolic interpretations? Stress the importance of recognizing potential symbolism, without its having to condition reading or response.

CHAPTER 5 NOTHING

1 📼

The poem seems to be a kind of 'farewell to love', a recognition of the passing of time, the end of *roving*, or adventuring, and the relationships implied.

1.1

Similarities: recurring gerunds, repeated phrases and words (*no more a-roving, loving, the moon*), rhymes in the first and third lines.
Differences: movement from night to day (the coming of dawn?), contrast between *So* (1) and *Yet* (11), rhymes in second and fourth lines. The second verse has a more hammering rhythm, created by the alliterative sounds of line 5 and by the prominent subject - verb - object pattern of the four lines as a whole.

1.2

So suggests this is a conclusion: something has led to the result that *we'll go no more a-roving*. It might also suggest acceptance of this fact, tying in with regret.

1.3

Open response. The first line is usually chosen by most readers, but any of lines 5 – 9 could be chosen too.

1.4

Open response. Usually the note of regret, of loss, is what strikes the reader most.

2 📼

The reflections go on, in the last two lines particularly, to wonder why the world exists at all – implying the futility of all existence.
The poem is a sonnet.

2.1

him = the dead soldier
its/it = the sun
this = the overall situation

2.2

At home (3) where he seems to have been a countryman, perhaps a farmer, who had to sow the fields. (There is an implied contrast here between the fruitful hope of sowing the fields, and the futile wasteland the soldier is now dying in.)

2.3

a *this morning* (5), contrasting with *always* (4) and *once* (2); *once* (9) refers back to the beginning of time.
b References to seeds and growing (see 3, 8) are linked to clay, from which the world is formed (9, 12).
c Line 1, an imperative, addressed, presumably, to unseen men, is reinforced by the lack of movement implied in lines 6 and 11.

2.4

Positive and warming at first, the sun's beams become futile and meaningless by the end of the poem.

2.5

Open response. To contrast with death, to stress the sun's powers of renewal, to stress life.

2.6

Probably the man has died and the command at line 1 has not had any reviving effect on him.

2.7

Open response. The contrast between positive and negative in the poet's attitude to the sun can be seen as balancing some of his desperation at the futility of it all.

2.8

Open response, deriving from previous questions: the sun's efforts are futile, as are all man's efforts.

2.9

Open response, but pretty clearly yes.

3 📼

Lines 5 – 8 imply a circular walking movement which contrasts with the emphasis on sitting, stiffness, and freezing in the rest of the poem.

3.1

Open response. Lines 1, 9, 10, and 13 are the most commonly chosen.

3.2

Open response, inviting readers to relate their own experience to the text. This can be delicate, so tact is called for: students may prefer to reflect, then perhaps write about such deeply affecting or even traumatic experiences, but the poem can be related to very effectively if the teacher does not shy away from its implications. (Some teachers may prefer to handle this question at a later stage.)

3.3

The heart (of the victim of the pain) wonders if Christ (*He* in 3) suffered in the same or a similar way, and if the pain is the same now and for all time, past and present.

3.4

Open response. Line 6 is lighter, anticipating the release of the very last words of the poem. *Ought* means 'nothing'.
Tombs/stiff/Quartz/stone/Lead all imply different aspects of weight, lying heavily on the victim of the pain.

3.5

Open response. They break the formal continuity without allowing the real pause that full stops might imply.

3.6

Open response.

4

He feels distanced, deliberately cut off from the outside world and no longer interested in it. Some readers find his attitude realistic, others selfish and cynical. NB Le Corbusier was arguably the most influential French architect of the twentieth century. Chartres cathedral, in France, is one of the most famous beautiful buildings in the world. Its architect's name is not known.

4.1

Open response. There are few clues in the text but lines 12 and 13, *I thought perhaps out here there would be enough pain and enough fear to distract*, perhaps suggest that the conversation takes place in Africa.

4.2

a The architect had nothing to prove and did not think of the judgement of posterity.
b All his preconceived ideas and beliefs began to fall apart, through one idea (one thread in the jacket) being questioned.

I am no Schweitzer (40) means 'I am not particularly charitable'. Dr Albert Schweitzer was a famous German missionary, founder of a leprosarium in Africa. He won the Nobel Prize for Peace in 1953.

4.3

a It will not last – someone else will take his place.
b The work did not deserve the money it earned him.
c He cannot love.
d He sees Rycker as representing disillusionment, boredom, resignation, and negative attitudes beyond his own. Students will need to imagine and conjecture about this one.

4.4

Open response. Reactions are generally ambiguous, and not particularly sympathetic.

4.5

Open response, which can lead to an evaluation of the importance of 'designer' labels, etc. on clothes, and the values these imply. Querry's view would be that the created work or product is more valuable than any 'name'.

4.6

Open response. The phrase *which of us are creative enough to 'make' love?* is usually picked out.

4.7

Summary. Aim for 10 – 15 words if possible.

5 🔲

He decides *to be* rather than *not to be*.
The soliloquy is in Act Three, Scene One, lines 56 to 88 of the play.

5.1

Positive: death = *a sleep*
Negative: life = *slings and arrows* (violent weapons), *a sea of troubles, heartache and natural shocks* (pain), *a calamity*
Death is also described as an *undiscovered country*, which could be either negative or positive.
Open response.

5.2

The *rub* is the negative aspect, i.e. dreams accompanying sleep. See 5.3.
The seven troubles in lines 15 – 19 could be summed up as: the harshness of time; of subjection; of others' arrogance; of rejected love; of the slowness of the law; of bureaucracy; and of people's worth going unrecognized while others, less able, make progress.
Open response.

5.3

Because the imagination is boundless, and the unknown is therefore terrifying.

5.4

In order:

is heir to	*fardels*
perchance	*bourn*
shuffled off this mortal coil	*hue*
calamity	*pitch and moment*
contumely	*currents*
quietus	*turn awry*
bodkin	

Open response.

5.5

Suggestions might include: awareness/self-awareness/fear of sin/fear of death or the unknown/ the inner voice of moral judgement/the fact or faculty of knowing and understanding/reflection/wish to behave correctly.
Hamlet decides for life, but with courage as well as some cowardice.
Open response.

CHAPTER 6 MONEY

Modern Prayer presents the rather cynical outlook of those who want to make money at all costs. The attitude of not caring about anyone who gets in the way confirms the self-interest of the speaker (who is **not** to be confused with the writer – he was using the narrative *me* to make a point **against** this kind of attitude).

Suggested adjectives: cynical, ruthless, ambitious, determined, callous, selfish, single-minded. The rhyme is the same throughout, strong and monosyllabic, underlining the strength of the speaker's words. The rhymes give the poem a stronger impact – especially the final very strong word!

Mammon is the god of riches.

1 📼

Open response. The speaker is serious but the poet himself isn't. Through the exaggerated attitude and opinions of 'the speaker' we detect the critical voice of the poet.

1.1

The café (verses 1 and 2); Town, i.e. London (verses 3 and 4); the theatre (verse 5); and a restaurant (verses 6 and 7).

1.2

pelf = money
cad = vulgar person
loll = recline
sup = eat
tipple = drink
scuttle = run quickly

1.3

en grand seigneur = like a lord
a crust to the poor = something small which costs nothing to give away
if ever so bad = no matter how bad it (the damage) is
be drunk as a lord = to be very drunk

1.4

Open response. Possible adjectives could be: arrogant, devil-may-care, snobbish, presumptuous, patronizing, boorish.

1.5

they = other people
we = rich people
it = spitting
it's = the performance

1.6

This requires the reader to go behind the superficial meaning – not everyone catches the intended irony. The exaggerated dismissiveness of the speaker in relation to other people – especially the poor (*a cad* at 21, for example) – seems to indicate that the poet is being ironic. His light-hearted irony conceals fairly strong feelings and social comment. Clough's ironic humour is refreshingly unexpected in Victorian poetry.

1.7

a The strongly emphasized rhyme scheme leads the reader on to catch the next unexpected choice of word, making the poem flow quickly.

b The rhythm, musical and light, adds to this a bouncy, light-hearted air.

c The refrain is the culmination of this effect, especially in *heigh-ho!*.

(As with other texts, the way this poem is read on the accompanying cassette could be evaluated. Has the reader caught the tone, is the humour there, is it light enough or too light-hearted, etc.? How would students prefer it to be read? Remember that the way any text is read on the cassette is just one interpretation, so the teacher, or anyone else, or another recording might give a better, or at least a different, reading/interpretation.)

1.8

The target would probably best be described as people who think themselves superior because they are rich, and the life-styles of such people.

2 📼

This passage is much more immediately accessible. Lack of money denies Gordon social, artistic, and sexual success.

2.1

thing = the rejection slip (7)
this = rejection
stupid thing = the sending of a poem of his to the *Primrose*

2.2

The setting is his bedroom. This comes out from lines 26 – 31, *this vile room* (31) making it clear. The aspidistra plant is symbolically the only decorative element in the room. *Dropping a card on Buckingham Palace* (16), means leaving his visiting card at the most famous royal home in London, as if he had a confidential relationship with the Royal Family. This self-directed sarcasm underlines the gulf Gordon feels existing between him and the *Primrose*.

2.3

Possible answers:
filled with hatred = *with wordless hatred* (1) and *he loathed* (3)
ashamed = *was acutely ashamed* (4)
disgusted = *loathly sleekness* (8)
furious = *a coterie . . . mother's milk* (18 – 19)
wounded = *that pansy crowd* (20)
angry = *the sods!* (21)
depressed = *a sense of deadly staleness* (29 – 30)
self-mocking = *ending in the lonely bed* (32 – 33)
embittered = *lack of money is at the bottom* (38)

2.4

snooty (10) = snobbish, arrogant, upper-class
highbrow (10) = with intellectual pretensions
coterie (18) = closed group, rather affected

pansy (20) = affected
mealy-mouthed (22) = not saying outright what you mean
Other examples:
sods (20 – 21) = a term of abuse
horn in (20) = join in without being invited
snubbed (35) = treated with contempt, ignored

2.5

Repetition reflects what is going on in Gordon's own mind, the tortuous self-torment that has been building up over *two years* (30).
If you have money you can move in cultured circles; you can *afford* culture.

2.6

Gordon, in his own mind. This is a kind of free direct speech.
The technique continues in *Wind the clock, set the alarm* (28 – 29) and *Money, money, all is money!* (34), i.e. in the present, rather than the past tense.

2.7

The first is dominated by anger and bitterness, directed outwards; the second by an unwilling resignation, tinged with self-pity, very much internalized.

a A verbal difference worth pointing out is between *tore … and flung* (5 – 6) and *crumpled up … threw it away* (26): as anger moves to resignation, the verbs are weaker.

b The repetitions become less angry too: compare *sods* (21, 25) with *failure* (37 – 38).

c His movements shift from the violent *flung* (6) to the mechanical *Wind the clock, set the alarm* (28).

d His unspoken thoughts settle into an old train rather than reflecting the anger of the moment which the rejection slip provoked.

3 🖳

This is one of the most famous moments in Dickens. *Until something turns up* (4) is well known, and originates from Mr Micawber.
Lines 14 – 15 contain two well-known proverbs.
Line 15 (*Take him for all in all . . .*) echoes a line from *Hamlet*.
A contradiction in what Mr Micawber says, is that he has failed to follow his own advice.

3.1

Open response.

3.2

They reveal the self-conscious putting on and off of attitudes, and allow the reader to observe the character from a distance, for a moment.

3.3

Not terribly fondly, although he tries to speak well of him. All Mr Micawber's attempts to praise him end rather weakly: his having good legs and eyes for his age (20 – 22) does not say much!
Mr Micawber seems to suggest that his father-in-law

hastened the marriage (*that maxim* [22] refers to *Procrastination is the thief of time.* [14]), but allocates no particular blame.

3.4

He is not sure of what he wants to say, but wants to make a good-sounding speech, hence his borrowings from proverbs, Shakespeare, and poetry (32 – 34). Hesitations are evident in lines 3, 7, 9 and 13. One of Mr Micawber's attractive qualities is that he reveals his character, his insecurity, and his own image of himself in his speech. Dickens' representation of it strikes us as authentic and natural.

3.5

Time.
Catch time before it passes; *carpe diem*.

3.6

A poetic effect expanding upon the *misery* resulting from profligacy. The effect is, however, slightly comic since the context of sentimentalized nature is far removed from the rest of the scene.
Note: the monetary terms in this extract are old pounds, shillings and pence.

4

Open response. Henry's preoccupation emerges in his very first words (3); *feared* (5); his feeling that he has been *disbursing* (10) (an unusual word for spending, paying out) all day, and on throughout the passage.

4.1

They get married at the Registry Office at *considerable* expense. They have the wedding-breakfast at Lyons' – ten shillings and seven pence. They go to Madame Tussaud's – no price mentioned. Now they are at the cinema in Kingsway – half a crown (two shillings and six pence, pre-decimal currency).

4.2

At Lyons' he is *frightened*, daunted by the surroundings, and worried by them too. At Madame Tussaud's his lavishness makes him feel like *a young millionaire*, while adoring his new wife (but he has already decided they will never do such things again). Now at the cinema he is very reluctant to part with the new one pound note in his pocket.
He has always lived poorly and cheaply; he has a shop at Riceyman Steps, and has never left his lowly surroundings before.

4.3

Dictionary work. *Canker* (26), *repast* (27), *enjoining* (50), *withal* (52), *watermarks* (55) should all be looked up, as they are fairly unusual.

4.4

Spending: *disbursing* (10); *flung its money about* (23); *conduct . . . his purse* (30).

4.5

Open response and discussion. He judges others' extravagance very negatively, distrusting people who have or who spend too much. His judgement of Violet's *true feminine capriciousness* (32 – 33) and his resolve *that this should be the last* (28) such trip show his determination and his attitude to his wife, which is, however, tempered by the line *A nice thoughtfulness on Violet's part.* (51)

The free indirect speech at lines 62 – 64 reveals that Violet can get her own way too, and the final lines show how sympathetically she has understood Henry's agony.

Violet is usually considered more sympathetic than Henry, who, in the view of most readers, is a little **too** preoccupied with not spending money.

4.6

Henry.

Similar moments of direct representation of Henry's feelings can be found in line 15 (*he was prepared to believe*), *really* (17), the exclamation mark at line 27, *if foolishly* (31), *No!* (40). The passage moves very cleverly through direct speech, free indirect speech, narrative report of thought (of both characters), and back to direct speech.

4.7

Open response.

5

This text should be handled slowly and carefully. Vocabulary problems are treated in 5.1 and 5.3, so the first reading/listening, and re-reading need only be used to find answers to the pre-reading stimulus. Possible answers: *shrine* (2); *saint* (2, 21); lines 3, 10, 13, 22.

5.1

mine = his gold (which is his soul, whereas the sun is the world's soul)

more glad = happier am I to view the splendour of my gold than *the teeming earth* is to see the sun

his = the sun's (splendour)

that = (the gold) which

this = the room where the scene is set

the best = *that age* (15), the Golden Age

thy looks = the looks of gold, attributed to Venus

dear saint = the gold, to which Volpone attributes divinity

he = *Who can get thee* (26), whoever acquires gold

5.2

He values gold even more highly than the sun.

a *his* (6) light is darkened by the gold, which shines like *a flame by night* or like *the day* shone out of the original darkness of the world (9 – 10)

b *The longed-for sun* (4) looks at the splendour of gold, and *son of Sol* (10 continuing to 11)

5.3

Greatly superior to any kind of pleasure.
Any ambition people have.
Money has power over everyone.
Everyone has his or her price, and can be bought.

5.4

Above all, an overwhelmingly selfish and single-minded devotion to money.

5.5

Open response.

5.6

They confirm the high value both characters put on wealth – it is worth more than wisdom, according to Mosca.

CHAPTER 7 IDENTITY

1

First impressions will catch the basic sense of the poem, particularly from the last verse.

Answers might be: a man drowning, an unhappy man, a misfit.

The questions that follow will extend this frame of reference.

1.1

Verse 1   poet/narrator (1 – 2); the drowning man (3 – 4)
Verse 2   bystanders, friends (5 – 7), i.e. *they* (see 8); poet/narrator (8)
Verse 3   the man (with a narrative parenthesis from the poet, 10) (9, 11– 12)

1.2

It negates the second verse.

1.3

much further out than you thought = too far from the beach
much too far out = out of his depth, i.e. unable to cope with social situations, or maybe even with life in general

1.4

The dead man viewed by the narrator, as opposed to the dead man in the first person.

1.5

Larking means joking, playing, laughing: *no no no* (9) seems to say that he did not love larking.

1.6

The poet/narrator's.
In order to confirm that the dead man is speaking in the rest of the verse.

1.7

Open response. All are relevant. Students may also find others and should justify their choice, opening up discussion on the impressions they now have of the poem.

1.8

Open response. Sympathy will go to the drowned man, almost invariably.

2 📟

This passage presents a different kind of social 'pretending'.
He is dependent on routine. He is narrow-minded. He doesn't like foreigners or foreign countries. He doesn't appreciate the Arts.

2.1

Satisfied, occurring three times (4, 5, 7), emerges as the most significant word. Repetition is an important part of Dickens's ironic technique in describing Mr Podsnap. The other adjectives – *well to do* (1), *brilliant* (6), and *thriven exceedingly* [= done very well] (3) – confirm his satisfaction, and might be suggested as secondary key-words.

2.2

Possible responses:

Paragraph 2: *Getting rid of disagreeables* (12) or *I don't want to know about it* (14 – 15)

Paragraph 3: *Not a very large world* (20); *Up at eight* (26, 31, 34, 38); *Swept away* (26); *Nothing else To Be* (42)

Paragraph 4: *What Providence meant* (46 – 47) or *Respectable* (47)

Paragraph 5: *Podsnappery* (53) or *Articles of a faith* (51)

2.3

Oral or written summary. Podsnap's self-centred view of the world, either eliminating these elements or subordinating them to his own limited view of life, will emerge. (This exercise can be done in three groups to save time, with each group summarizing a different aspect.)

2.4

Mr Podsnap's business being *sustained* (22), or kept alive, by contact with other countries.

2.5

Mr Podsnap's name, as well as many nouns, adjectives, and adverbs will emerge as repeated. So will key-words, especially the sequence of getting up/shaving close/breakfasting/going to the City/coming home/dining, in the third paragraph.
Echoes include the use of sounds and occasional alliterations for a slight effect of repetition: the use of 'c' sounds in lines 22 – 24 is a good example. The repetition of Mr Podsnap's daily routine is, of course, the high point of this technical use of repetition.

2.6

quite satisfied (4)
happily (9)
a grand convenience (12)
lofty (14)
Elsewise (26)
close (27)
required, under his protection (45)
exactly (46)
comfortable (49)
Students may pick out several others.

2.7

A few examples, among others:
inheritance (2)
thriven exceedingly (3)
acquainted (9)
dignified conclusiveness (11)
affronted(19)
sustained (22)
respectively (30)
Professors (34)
sedately (38)
vagrants (41)

2.8

Open response.

3 📟

The change is between the two paragraphs; the first recounts the metamorphosis, the second the narrator's reactions and reflections.

3.1

Summary. The visual elements are contained in lines 1 – 8: he is seen to drink, reel, stagger, clutch at the table, stare, then change and swell, his face blackening as *the features seemed to melt and alter*.

3.2

A cry (1); *gasping (3)*; *screamed (9)*.

3.3

His movements (6 – 7) and the terror he feels, which leads him to scream (9), reveal the depth of his shocked reaction. This is confirmed by such phrases as *my soul sickened* (14 – 15) and lines 16 – 19 and 21 – 22.

3.4

Open response. Discussion of how the scene could be acted or filmed will bring out elements of exaggeration or simplicity. Usually readers find the scene surprisingly simple and economical in its effects. Comparison with Poe's *The Black Cat* might bring out similarities/differences in style and effect. The last line of the present text shows that Mr Hyde, the real Doctor Jekyll's *alter ego*, is a notorious murderer.

3.5

Open discussion.

3.6

Open discussion. The duality of good and bad in all of us might be the conclusion. (cf. Poe again.)

4

A complete short story for extensive reading.

4.1

Mischief: lines 21, 32, 45 – 46, 49, 50, 65, 91 – 92,
101 – 102
Punishment: lines 20, 25, 33 – 35, 43, 47, 48,
49 – 50, 67, 92, 103

4.2

In effect, all the other things he did! (103 onwards.)

4.3

a lines 37 – 38, 84, 91, 137 – 138, 149 – 151
b lines 35 – 38, 71, 143

4.4

It stands for an organization, but could be expressed as 'a
meeting between parents and teachers'.
The full name is Parent-Teachers Association.

4.5

Middle-class American, probably in a fairly small town (no
traffic, tea and cakes, walking to school, hills, muddy
garden).
kindergarten = first level of instruction after nursery school
fresh = disrespectful, impertinent
cookie = biscuit
gee = informal expression of surprise, concern, etc.
color = American spelling of 'colour'
first grade = first class or 'form' at school after kindergarten
            (*kindergarten to 12th grade* = from 5 to 17 years
            of age)
rubbers = waterproof overshoes, galoshes
More expressions:
to take the name of the Lord in vain (13) = mention God's
name unnecessarily (Puritan heritage)
Look up, Look down, etc. (35 – 38) = typical of
children's lore
recess (47) = break
Hi, Pop, y'old dust mop. (71) = over-confidential address
clearly chosen by Laurie for its rhyming effect

4.6

grimly = sternly, gloomily, for there was nothing exciting
about Charles's good behaviour
haggard = tormented, having suffered through Charles's
bad behaviour
primly = in a very formal, precise way
warily = cautiously, not believing his ears
elaborately = in a studied way, because she didn't want to
upset Laurie with her questions
respectfully = impressed with Charles's courage

4.7

The use of *fresh* (21 and elsewhere) to mean mischievous;
He sure did (35); *Gee* (37); *he wasn't let* (92). Students may
find and discuss others.

4.8

Because he (as Charles) created so many problems. The
teacher is being very polite, however, and does not reveal
her true feelings.

4.9

Open response.

4.10

Open response.

5 📼

There is a lot of unusual vocabulary in this poem, but it is
one which always provokes an interested and committed
response. No vocabulary anticipation is necessary; it will be
handled later. The poem is an example of being wise
before the event – a voice of 'experience' which cannot
have had the experience. The speaker is an unborn child.

5.1

Open response. Lines 5 – 6, 25 – 26, 32 and the last two
lines are particularly accessible and striking.

5.2

The answers may be the same as were given for 5.1. The
positive lines are few: lines 8 – 11 are the only real
examples.

5.3

This is the core question for comprehension of the poem,
but it is worth stressing that some lines will remain a little
obscure and ambiguous no matter how closely they are
examined (15 – 17, for example). Dictionary work will lead
to evaluation of connotations. Open response.

Lines
2 – 3   images of evil or fearsome beasts or spirits
5 – 7   images of imprisonment, enticement and
         temptation, and torture
9 – 11   images of ease, pleasure (*dandle* is very
         unusually used here – it usually means 'to dance a
         child on your knees'; the sense is of pleasurable,
         comforting support), nature, and a sense of
         direction
13 – 17 images of sin, betrayal, instrumentalization, and
         being forced to act against one's will
19 – 24 images of behaviour, roles, social pretence, fear
         and inhibition, scorn and rejection
26 – 27 images of inhumanity and supreme arrogance
29 – 37 images of reaction and opposition, rejection of
         unwanted roles, diminution of identity, lack of
         solidity
38 – 39 conclusion

5.4

a 8 – 11   b 28 – 37   c 18 – 24
d 12 – 17   e 1 – 3   f 8 – 11

5.5

Open response. The effect of listing is vital, but the
movement is from solid to vulnerable (33 – 37 are the best

reflection of this close connection between sound and sense). The rhyme (largely on *me*) is highly irregular.

5.6 ——————————————

Open response. This is a delicate subject and should be handled with care. A class debate might be organized. 'Justification' of abortion is not the poet's intention: the poem is more about life than death.

CHAPTER 8 IN AND OUT OF TIME

1 🖭

First impressions will probably already bring in ideas of life, death, and transience. The Latin title is translated at 1.6.

1.1 ——————————————

Open response. He is more resigned than anything else.

1.2 ——————————————

Line 2 contains abstracts; the weeping and the laughter are more concrete and tangible.

1.3 ——————————————

we pass the gate = death
our path = life

1.4 ——————————————

More hedonistic certainly: therefore it could possibly be seen as more positive.

1.5 ——————————————

Life, emerging from uncertainty, and dying into further uncertainty.

1.6 ——————————————

Open response.

1.7 ——————————————

Open response.

2 🖭

These two poems can be presented separately or together, although it will probably be easier to take them one at a time.
The theme is love and loss, or probable loss, so the attitudes could be described as positive, in spite of the threat or fact of ending.

2.1 ——————————————

It is not clear from the poem: the *you* may or may not be present.
The *I* is addressing the *you* directly, and they are clearly lovers, and have been for some time.
The time (5) seems to be some time ago in the writer's memory.

2.2 ——————————————

Open response. The answers (oral or written) should bring out the contrast between lines 3 and 4 to the end.
Possible answer: on your leaving I will still have this one

memory to treasure.

2.3 ——————————————

Open response. Students usually prefer a version with an English title, simply because it is more accessible. Some find the Latin title pretentious.

2.4 ——————————————

The first words could have been spoken either by the speaker of the poem, *me* (4), or by *she* (1). The proximity of *she* to the statement makes her the more likely speaker. However, the second half of the poem (4 – 7) confirms the poet's gratitude also, so it is to be hoped that the feeling was mutual.
One hour (5). Students might want to discuss whether this hour is literally an hour or is used figuratively to stand for an unstated length of time.

2.5 ——————————————

The simile contains beauty and vulnerability (*hanging flowers*, 2), movement and change (*wind . . . lifted . . . aside*, 3), brightness (*the ray of sun*, 2) – echoing the woman's beauty, her going, the joy of the moment before she went.

2.6 ——————————————

There is a sense of identification with the gods, in that the poet's experience transcends human things and he equates his hour with heavenly joy. The words *hath* (3) and *Nay* (4) confirm, in their old-fashioned Biblical tones, a heightened sensation, as does the echo of epic in the simile. The gods are eternal, not specifically religion-based, and the poet has shared and described an eternal moment. Discussion might arise on how we often make reference to 'heaven' in the context of pleasure and happy memories. Is this true in the students' own language?

2.7 ——————————————

The poems share a capacity to remember the best moments of the relationships they describe. *When You Go* uses a very specific moment, related in detail. *Erat Hora* uses a simile for the loss, rendering it beautiful in itself, and evokes the gods by way of confirming the memory of the moment, which is, however, left undescribed. Morgan's moment is explicit, Pound's implicit, but the memories will remain because of the retention of the joy of the high points of the relationships.

3 🖭

Reference is almost exclusively to present time. *Hereafter* (2) refers to a hypothetical future; *to-morrow* (4) and *all our yesterdays* (7) are referred to in relation to the effect of future and past time on present time.

3.1 ——————————————

An insect, or an animal: the connotations are low, furtive, animal.
Syllable (6) is usually associated with words, perhaps also vocalized sound; *recorded* (6) with memory, history, sound, knowledge.
Similar unexpected collocations might be: *yesterdays* (7)

with *lighted* (7); an interesting contrast is that between *candle* (8) and *shadow* (9), and between *struts and frets* (10) and *a poor player* (9).

3.2

Life in general.
Lighted.

3.3

Life is seen as a brief *appearance*, a momentary performance preceded and followed by darkness, all ultimately meaningless.
Response may lead to open discussion.

3.4

Open response.

4

The reader becomes involved (*probably the reader can imagine*, 4) in the changing of the seasons; then the moon and night and day are brought in before the abrupt change to stress how time can also stand still or pass very quickly.

4.1

unfurl = open up
sickle = thin as a curved blade
lodges = is contained
queer = strange
discrepancy = gap/difference
directly = the moment . . . / as soon as
round and fill = swell
odds and ends = small unimportant objects

4.2

No.
The author has deliberately played with time. The last sentence of the passage is a good example of this.

4.3

People are able to move freely in time, at least in their minds, while animals and vegetables are more tied to the rhythm of the seasons. (See 16 – 18 in particular.) So time is different for people, more flexible, and possibly also more problematic.

4.4

We can tell very little, apart from his mental preoccupation with time and the passing of time or the nature of time: this is the real theme of the passage.

4.5

Open response.

5

This poem presents some cultural difficulties in that there is a range of references to classical Greek culture. (*Attic shape* [41] refers, for example, to Attica, the region of Ancient Greece whose culture has come down to us most significantly.)
Grecian, rather than 'Greek', poetically evokes the tradition of classical culture, and the artistic values that culture embodied for Keats. The urn, with its decoration, can be seen as symbolizing eternal beauty, and, therefore, eternal truth.
The poem is a great affirmation of the value of beauty, and, thereby, of life, although 5.9. allows for discussion of opposing views.
Students will find images of music in lines 10, 11 – 16, 23 – 24; love in lines 8 – 9, 17 – 20, 25 – 30; time in lines 2, 46 – 50.

5.1

Because it relates a tale of the countryside, with flowers and leaves, far from the town (see 35).

5.2

That it is peopled with human beings and/or gods engaged in some kind of chase, or at least following one another. Joy and music are also shown.

5.3

Physical, audible music is contrasted with music which appeals to a kind of 'inward ear'.

5.4

a He can never move in place or time, but neither can she; he can never reach her, but they will never lose their perfection.
b *canst not* (15 – 17); *ever* (16); *never, never* (17); *cannot fade* (19); *For ever* (20)
c Real lovers age, spring turns to autumn, beauty fades – the lovers on the urn need never suffer these things. Real lovers suffer sorrow, pain, longing, perhaps disappointment or boredom, in any case, the anticlimax of passion – these do not.

5.5

A scene of religious rite and sacrifice, with many more people in it.

5.6

Lines 35 – 40, describing and addressing the imagined town.

5.7

a At line 41 the poet moves from description of (or inspired by) the urn to reflections provoked by it.
b The timelessness, not only of the urn, but of beauty in general.
c The urn, directly addressed, takes us out of our normal mundane thoughts and onto a level of thought which considers eternity. The urn is cold, the scene pastoral: it is eternal. It thus makes us lose the thread of our own thoughts: our mind becomes dizzy. The silent presence

of the urn perplexes, puzzles, and teases us, posing problems: it fascinates and worries us at the same time.

5.8 _____

The speaker is a poet (*our*) and a mortal (*us, this*).
He seems to coincide with Keats.

5.9 _____

Open response. Students often reject what they take to be the main idea of the poem, i.e. a refusal to act, to live life to the full; they will tend to dismiss Keats as 'decadent' in his attitude to life. In particular they often do not accept Keats' concept of love as expressed here. Discussion might explore these issues.

CHAPTER 9 ALONE

1 📼

This poem may be greeted with some mystification on first reading, but as soon as students get the reference to tennis, all should become clear. The title refers to a tennis score (*love* having the extra meaning of 'zero'), as well as to romance in middle age. The layout places the net between the two participants.

1.1 _____

Open response. It is important that the poem can be about anything from tennis to an unhappy marriage: it is all a question of interpretation.

1.2 _____

Possibly the poems in Chapter 1. Comparisons might be brought out.

1.3 _____

Open response.

2 📼

Students will find that almost the whole poem is positive: even the concept of loneliness is redeemed here.

2.1 _____

Flowers: *fluttering* (6), *dancing* (6), *tossing* (12)
Waves: *danced* (13), *sparkling* (14)
The imagery of joy, light, freedom, space, infinity, is created.
Open response.
The verbs used of the poet, *wandered, saw, gazed,* and *lie* all suggest slowness or stillness and so they highlight the contrast between him and the flowers and waves.

2.2 _____

The pleasure described in the final verse; the memory which *oft* (19) returns to the poet of the sight of the daffodils.
The first sight of the daffodils makes him happy and the memory of it brings him recurring joy.

2.3 _____

The joy of being alone.
The mind's eye, i.e. what you can see only in your own mind, the imagination.

2.4 _____

Open response.
Themes: loneliness; the beauty of nature; man's response to nature; the power of the imagination.

2.5 _____

Open response. This allows for discussion of subjectivity and objectivity, and for comparison of students' experience to that of the poet.

3 📼

3.1 _____

It gives a sense of anonymity – we do not know who *she* is. This is presumably part of the desired effect in the poet's writing.

3.2 _____

Half-hidden (6), *only one* (7), *unknown* (9), *few* (9), *ceas'd to be* (10) might all be suggested.
Positive counterparts might be: *well-frequented; many, some; well-known/familiar; many; lived*.
The second part of the question will reveal readers' intuitions as to what Lucy lacked – she has some love, but no fame.
There is no evidence that she was necessarily deprived or unhappy – she may have been happy in her relationship with the poet (or the narrative voice of the poem). Students usually take her general situation as negative, however, especially in the present context of solitude and loneliness. It is worth pointing out that the poem is about her death, rather than the negative aspects of her life.

3.3 _____

A violet, because it is a flower that tends to keep its beauty concealed, and a star.

3.4 _____

Open discussion. The effect of anonymity might be lessened if the poem had *Lucy* as its title.

3.5 _____

Brief summary, preferably oral.
The Dove is a river between Staffordshire and Derbyshire; *the springs of Dove* are the sources of the river in the remote hills of the Peak District.
Open response.

3.6 _____

Open imaginative response. The positive possibilities should be stressed as much as possible. The present loss (12) should give the idea of a very close relationship in the past.

3.7 _____

Open response, bringing together the conclusions drawn from the last three questions.

3.8

Common elements: content with rural solitude; lack of public fame.
Differing elements: she is dead while the speaker in Pope's text is alive; Wordsworth tells a story, Pope expresses a wish.
Open response.

4 ▣

Reading the second half of the story first will allow students more freedom of intuition and interpretation of the character of the woman whose story it is. The title should not be revealed, as the suggestions in response to the pre-reading stimulus will lead to the idea of a pet, or some kind of dumb companion, with recognition that it is a canary coming later, in the second paragraph. See also 4.7.

4.1

It has died.

4.2

It was her only real companion.
Possible adjectives: dependent, familiar, trusting, understanding, conversational, sympathetic, cosy, even perhaps loving.

4.3

There is no direct explicit addressee. The conversational style presupposes an interlocutor who is in the house of the speaker. Open response.

4.4

he = the canary
that = company
them = *my three young men* (lodgers presumably)
him = the canary
this = what she is saying or has just said
it = the bad dream
they = people
it = something sad in life

4.5

Open response, depending on attitudes to pets.
The washerwoman clearly thinks a dog would be better company, more comfort.

4.6

Open response, deriving from previous questions.

4.7

Open response. The correct title, *The Canary*, can be revealed and evaluated only **after** this discussion.

4.8

The first part fills in more of the background circumstances of the story, which is now complete. (The use of a series of full stops at the beginning of the first sentence does not indicate cutting, but hesitation in the first person narrator's speech.)

4.9

after my time = when she leaves the house (or, possibly, dies)
the next people = the next tenants of the house
he = the canary
The cage hung from the nail.

4.10

The house, the garden, flowers, the evening star. These are never 'enough' compared to the canary, which seems to communicate with her right from its first *faint, small chirp* (38).

4.11

Open response.
Sentimental and lonely may be the ideas that predominate. She lives her loneliness in resignation, sadness, solitude, and memories.

4.12

Open response and discussion.
The important thing is that she herself **thinks** she has *a cheerful disposition*, and this is enough, psychologically, to keep her going.

4.13

Open response/summary.

5 ▣

It will be better if students proceed directly to the two verses extrapolated. The poem is introduced slowly. Students will be able to identify several elements: the water (*sea*), the ship (*boards*), and thirst (last line of the first verse). The next verse gives the idea of repetition, stasis. A speaker (or speakers) is introduced: *we*, the crew. A picture is created in the last two lines. Something awful has happened, and the ship and its crew are being punished. The pre-reading text may be referred to now, before students go on to read the prose commentary. Thus they will have had a taste of the ballad rhythm and the poetic description in the verses, and will notice the straightforward, uninvolved tone of the margin commentary. (This, incidentally, did not appear in the first edition – in *Lyrical Ballads*, 1798 – but was added by Coleridge for a later edition.) Clearly the Ancient Mariner is speaking. His feelings might contain regret, a feeling of obsession with what has happened, a need to talk about it, in order to exorcize it.

5.1

The commentary gives a different note, an outsider's summary which talks of *a spirit*, thus introducing another element of spiritual mystery, to offset the first-person narrative.

5.2

The vivid clarity of the images and the sounds of the verse make almost all the images striking!
Open response.

5.3

The words are given in the order in which they appear:

hid (3) = concealed, shrouded
hellish (9) = infernal, evil
woe (10) = trouble, anguish
averred (11) = asserted, said
wretch (13) = miserable creature
slay (13) = kill
dim (15) = unclear, rather dark
uprist (16) = rose
'twas (19) = it was
foam (21) = wave-tops
furrow (22) = the ship's wake
burst (23) = arrived, penetrated
dropt (25) = fell, lowered
copper (29) = deep metallic red/brown
mast (31) = central support for sails
stuck (34) = remained still
idle (35) = immobile
shrink (38) = become dry, contract

5.4

Corruption: *rot* (41); *slimy things* (43)
Evil spell: *witch's oils* (47); *the spirit* (50)

5.5

Open response. An evil destiny or a vengeful presence are the most common interpretations.
The commentary makes it more definite, more of a scientifically attested spirit.

5.6

They are six-line verses, with added repetitions. Lines 23 and 24, which reach a kind of euphoria.

5.7

a time indicators, conjunctions (*now, and, then,* etc.), most of the past-tense verbs
b descriptions of sun, wind, silence, etc.
c first person *I* (9 – 11, 17, etc.)
d lines 11, 17, 19, 49

6

It is important to take this extract in reverse, so as to build up students' awareness of the situation. Lines 57 – 78 are read first; 42 – 56 before question 6.7; 22 – 41 before question 6.9; and the whole text, including lines 1 to 21, before question 6.11.

6.1

Gently (58) *gentler* (60)

6.2

Noiselessly slid (63); *tremor* (76); *retired* (77).
They give a slightly sinister impression of reserve, hidden emotion, and a will not to exist.

6.3

Open response.
This is intended to encourage speculation, and a kind of prediction. Clearly they are master and employee. Perhaps the employer wants to know Bartleby's background in order to have an idea of who to contact if anything should happen to Bartleby.
The narrator is a lawyer. The *bust of Cicero* (71) is the head of the most famous Roman classical orator, statesman and lawyer, Marcus Tullius Cicero (106 – 43 BC), famous for his polished and eloquent style which helped him win legal and political cases in the time of Julius Caesar. Perhaps there is a subtle hint that the classical lawyer's capacities as an interrogator were greater than the present narrator's!

6.4

To clear up a sense of mystery surrounding him. *Gently* and *gentler* (already noted in 6.1), *I feel friendly towards you* (68 – 69), and *after waiting a considerable time* (73 – 74).

6.5

He is retiring, isolated, enclosed – like a hermit.

6.6

Bartleby's reticence, immovability, and silence – even when he moves – create mystery and uncertainty.
The narrator's continued attempts to get him to answer questions might reveal some frustrations, which might in turn lead to tension.

6.7

Words like *calm* (46) and lines 51 – 56 confirm the narrator's sympathy and concern, and give us a clearer insight into the questioning of Bartleby.
The concern is partly due to professional uncertainty, partly normal humanity.

6.8

Open response. Speculation, before further reading.

6.9

Much now becomes clear. His employer is worried about Bartleby living in the office (*he made my office his constant abiding place and home*, 23) and about his psychological peculiarities.
We still do not know what the narrator *had seen* (43).

6.10

I
a prudential feeling (25)
melancholy (26)
pity (27)
fear (29)
repulsion (29)
his soul I could not reach (41)
Bartleby
morbid moodiness (24)
forlornness (27)
victim of innate and incurable disorder (39)
it was his soul that suffered (40 – 41)
noiselessly slid into view (63)

6.11 _____

The mystery of Bartleby remains unresolved, but the reasons for the narrator's concern are now clear. See 6.9 and 6.10.

Additions to the list made in 6.10:

I
awed me into my tame compliance (16 – 17)
had feared to ask him (17 – 18)

Bartleby
pallid haughtiness (15)

Bartleby might just possibly be out for a walk at the moment.

6.12 _____

Open response. The narrator did what Bartleby wanted, and did so humbly, because of the effects of Bartleby's seemingly superior air.

6.13 _____

Open response.

6.14 _____

Open response: prediction.

6.15 _____

Open response: discussion and evaluation.

Graffiti Greta Garbo and Mae West are famous cinema stars, the former well known for her reluctance to let people intrude into her privacy, the latter for her frantic social life.

CHAPTER 10 EMOTIONS AND FEELINGS

1 🖾 _____

A little (very little) background on the First World War (1914 – 1918) would not go amiss. Bring out the fact that although (perhaps because) it was the worst war in history until that time it brought forth a flood of great poetry. Clearly, the beauty of the singing 'wins' over the horrors (undescribed but implicit) of the war. Discussion might arise, here or later, as to whether the poem's effect would be different if students had not been told of the First World War context.

1.1 _____

The immediate answer is *Everyone* (1, 6, 9), but lines 9 – 10 tell us that *Everyone was a bird*, i.e. only a bird was singing. The human voices remain eternal, like birdsong.

1.2 _____

Line 3 and the end of line 5 in particular suggest escape. They start slowly from the prison, using a simile and developing the idea of freedom in *Winging wildly* (4) until the point of view changes: above and away. Notice also that the last line of each verse breaks the shape of the poem, as if to confirm the flight of the escaped bird.

This escape takes the poet out of his (undescribed) situation. The suddenness and completeness of the release underscores the implication of the heaviness of the

imprisonment that existed before. Only at line 8 does he reveal *horror* in his present situation: escape from that horror is the vital joy of the singing – and the motivation for writing the poem.

1.3 _____

The surrounding situation, and so the speaker's/poet's initial state of mind. *Prisoned birds* (3) can be read negatively. *Horror*, if we had no knowledge of the background to the text, might come as a shock and might colour a generally positive impression.

1.4 _____

This is an appeal to the emotions: sudden joy in sadness can be very moving. Elicit students' response to the possibility of being moved in such a situation. Discuss why the poet was so moved. Is the reader likely to be similarly moved or is he or she automatically excluded by objectivity from such close involvement?

1.5 _____

The **effect** of the singing continues, so the singing continues too, at least to an extent. The singing is an aspect of the eternal which is revealed to the poet in the midst of the *horror* (8).

The poem can be seen, then, as a revelation, conveying something which will never end – which rises above the prison, the horror, etc. Students might want to go deeper into this contrast between high and low, eternal and mundane.

1.6 _____

Open response.

2 _____

Another complete short story for extensive reading. The computer turns out to be the hero, and the story of *true love* is his/its. This should not be revealed yet, however!

2.1 _____

Opening (1 – 14)
Exposition (14 – 19)
Search, in four stages (20 – 32, 33 – 39, 39 – 51, 52 – 88)
Analysis of Milton, and growth of Joe (89 – 124)
Finding Charity (125 – 135)
Reversal (sting in the tail) (139 – 153)

2.2 _____

Age: 25 – 40
IQ: over 120
Height: 150 – 175 cm
No children living
Not red-haired
English-speaking

2.3 _____

Open response. This is designed to create an objective reading sense, through recall of reaction during reading.

2.4 _____

Open response.
The turning point is in line 139, *they came to arrest him*, or line 144, *He's gone*.

2.5 _____

Open response. The most likely answers are **a**, **g**, and **h**.

2.6 _____

Summary.

3 ▣ _____

This is another First World War poem, but the tone of resignation and disenchantment is almost the opposite of Sassoon's.

3.1 _____

destiny = *fate*
defend, fight for = *guard*
probable = *likely*
I won't be missed by people at home = *no (likely) end could bring them loss*
forced to fight = *bade me fight*
shouting encouragingly = *cheering*
loud noise = *tumult*
useless, pointless = *waste of breath*

3.2 _____

Open response. *A lonely impulse of delight* (11), the solitary thrill of flying and his balancing of past/future, life/death led him to volunteer.
He is possibly at the airfield, and may soon be taking off.
The clouds above might suggest such an interpretation.
Some readers prefer the idea that he is in Kiltartan, on a final visit.

3.3 _____

Lines 3 and 4 use both repetition (*Those that I . . ./I do not . . .*), and contrast (*fight/guard, hate/love*). *My country/ my countrymen* uses partial repetition, reinforced by the place name, repeated in lines 5 – 6. *Nor*, repeated four times in lines 9 – 10, gives an unusual negative stress to reasons that he denies for becoming the airman/fighter he now is. The very close repetition (14 – 15) of *waste of breath* leads to the balance of the last line, and, particularly the last four words.
This balance of contrasts gives the idea of solid, careful judgement in a difficult, and, indeed, ambiguous situation.
The title, with *foresees* might suggest something supernatural, but the poem is totally rational, depending on the first verb, *I know*. There is little emotion, no patriotism.
In short, reason confirms the complete absence of the kind of reactions we might normally expect in the face of death.
(A useful contrasting text might be Hamlet's soliloquy, *To be or not to be*, in Chapter 5, where similar techniques of contrast and balance are used, but with the aim of argument rather than statement or affirmation, as is the case here.)

3.4 _____

Kiltartan Cross, his home village in Ireland, and its people (5 – 7) are the only localized references. The *I* speaking dominates the poem, but lines 9 – 10 open up the frame of reference, as do lines 3 – 4, bringing in friends, enemies, and a wider public.
Personal, private feelings are all considered (13) and balanced with the **absence** of public commitment in the airman's final, highly personal decision.
Open response.

3.5 _____

Summary. This need only be brief, but balanced.

4 ▣ _____

A black person is speaking in an assertive tone, proud of his/her colour, and challenging whites.

4.1 _____

Any black person: therefore it could also be Hughes himself (see The Authors).
It is not actually important to know that the poet was black.

4.2 _____

Yes: *brother* (2) is male, and his expression of how whites treat him indicates a more adult social awareness.

4.3 _____

Open response.

4.4 _____

too = as well as the white person/the reader
the darker brother = darker than the (white) brother
they = his masters (whites)
company = other people (whites)

4.5 _____

I	They
am the darker brother	send me to eat in the kitchen
Now	*Tomorrow/Then*
I laugh, eat well and grow strong	I'll sit at the table
	They won't dare send me away
	They'll see how beautiful I am
	They'll be ashamed

4.6 _____

Open response. As the lists above confirm, the idea of contrast, and perhaps conflict, dominates.

4.7 _____

Open response. Hughes lived from 1902 to 1967. This poem dates from the early 1930s.
Students usually consider it highly relevant to today.
Special mention might be made of the situation in South Africa.

4.8 _____

Open response. All the descriptions are valid in some way, but most students will probably stress the political aspects of the poem. The speaker's strength will probably be seen as necessary for the assertion of his rights. *They* will be *ashamed* at having denied a fellow human being social equality.

4.9 _____

Open response. The best single word might be 'committed' but, of course, there can be many others in a situation caused by what the Scottish poet Robert Burns called 'man's inhumanity to man', the oppression of a minority. Discussion can be extended to bring out, for example, prejudices within a country or race: north/south, rich/poor, employed/unemployed, old/young, fashionable/unfashionable, straight/gay, beautiful/ugly, town/country, metropolis/provinces, Catholic/Protestant, etc. etc.

5 📼

5.1 _____

It is torture by terror rather than by physical pain, so is more psychological.
This is possibly more effective than physical torture in that the victim is kept in a state of terrified uncertainty.

5.2 _____

Smell: *the foul musty odour* (38); touch: *the wire brushed his cheek* (56), and, some might say, Winston's thoughts, which almost become part of what he feels, especially just before his final outburst.

5.3 _____

O'Brien speaks *didactically* (8) to the *invisible audience* providing a kind of detached objective commentary which adds to Winston's sufferings: the objective reinforces the purely subjective psychological terror he is undergoing, so that when he becomes *helpless, mindless,* O'Brien's intervention (54) brings him back to brutal reality.

5.4 _____

Probably Winston himself. It only *seemed to come from outside himself.*
It would be a reaction to the sounds of the rats (and to O'Brien's *lecture*).

5.5 _____

Because if the mind dies, everything is given up. The alternative is surrender.

5.6 _____

Because his terror is of the violence the rats would do to **his** body – the best escape is to substitute someone else's body.
This turns out to be Julia's body for Winston's at the end of the passage, as the repeated imperative, *Do it to Julia!* confirms.

5.7 _____

Probably with Winston's last words, O'Brien has won and can stop the torture.
Open response. Usually students imagine Winston's remorse and self-reproach in directing the torture away from himself and towards Julia. He will now be in O'Brien's power.

5.8 _____

Open response. But tact may be necessary!

5.9 _____

Winston's love affair with Julia is almost the only positive note in the whole of the novel, so his betrayal of her now is all the more shocking, emphasizing how the State (symbolized by O'Brien) can dominate and, indeed, can render utterly subordinate, every aspect of the individual. Open response.

6 📼

We conclude on a note of overwhelming joy – but a joy that the writer/speaker seems to imply that humankind is incapable of reaching.

6.1 _____

They build up to a crescendo of *joy*, musically adding to the visionary effect.

6.2 _____

Summary. The unselfconscious freedom of the fish contrasts with the limiting self-concern of people.

6.3 _____

Open reaction and response. Although silence and reflection might be the best reaction to such a vision.

INDEX OF AUTHORS